The Essence of Healing

A Guide to the Alaskan Essences

2nd Edition

Lesley —
May the healing power of
alaska bless you and
yours!   *Steve*

by
Steve Johnson

Published by:

Alaskan Flower Essence Project

PO Box 1369, Homer, Alaska 99603
Tel: 1-800-545-9309 (U.S. & Canada)
Outside U.S. & Canada: 907-235-2188
Fax: 907-235-2777

Email: info@alaskanessences.com
Web: www.alaskanessences.com

ISBN: 0-9635584-2-0

Front cover photo:
Denali - © 2000 Calvin Hall/Alaskastock.com
Inside photo credits:
Greenland Icecap - Keri Petersen
Northern Lights - © 2000 Calvin Hall/AlaskaStock.com
Polar Ice - Doug Buchanan
Rainbow Glacier - Shabd-sangeet Khalsa
All other photos © 2000 Steve Johnson

Printed in Canada
Printed on Recycled Paper

Table of Contents

Acknowledgments

I would like to acknowledge the following people for their help in bringing the Alaskan essences and this book into being. Their spirit of adventure, resourcefulness, and enthusiasm has been greatly appreciated at every step along the way. My profound thanks to: Shabd-sangeet Khalsa, Janice Schofield, Doug Buchanan, Keri Petersen, Leonie FitzGerald, Debra Chesnut, Ruth Toledo, and Jane Bell.

I would especially like to express my gratitude to Jane for her clarity, perspective, and loving support throughout the writing of this book, for the research she has done on all of the Alaskan essences, and for her dedication to the task of bringing forth the full potential of vibrational healing to the world.

I would also like to give thanks to the plant, mineral, elemental, and devic kingdoms for their unconditional love, energy, and wisdom. Their constant support has made this book possible.

Preface to the Second Edition

Welcome to the second edition of The Essence of Healing – A Guide to the Alaskan Essences.

I am happy to announce that this new edition features color photos of all 72 of the flowers contained in our **Practitioner Kit**, and of the 12 essences in our **Environmental Kit**.

Below each picture are two affirmations. These positive statements are offered to expand your understanding of the message contained within each essence. They can also be used to enhance your receptivity to the healing energies of the essences.

The work of researching essences is an ongoing, living process. This edition contains additional information on the healing qualities of the essences collected during the four years since the publication of the original version. Sources include our yearly Training Program held here in Alaska, workshops conducted in many different countries of the world, feedback sent to us from clients and therapists, and from the experiences of remaking the essences.

I have also included a new section on our **Combination Formulas** and **Sacred Space Sprays**, exciting new products that have been released within the past two years. And at the very back of the book you will find the latest information available on all of the research essences in our repertory.

Foreword

I was born in Idaho, in the Rocky Mountain region of the western United States. In my childhood I was blessed by the fact that my parents owned a remote parcel of land along the Salmon River in the eastern part of the state. I spent many a summer day there playing among the tall pine trees, swimming in the river, and communing in a child's way with those I now know as the ensouling intelligences of nature: the devas and elementals.

After graduating from high school in 1971 I took a job as a forest fire fighter in the central Idaho wilderness. This work allowed me to deepen my relationship to the natural world in many ways. Most importantly, it repeatedly brought me into a position where I could witness and be a part of the intense interplay of the elemental energies that accompany a forest fire.

In 1978 I was offered a fire fighting position in Alaska which I readily accepted. Coming to Alaska was my entrance into a graduate course of nature study. The dance of elemental energies that I had enjoyed in my summers in the wild country of Idaho seemed to pale in comparison to what I was able to experience in this great land. Everything here was presented on a grand scale—the endless miles of wilderness, the massive storms, fires exceeding the scope and intensity of any I had witnessed before, and, of course, acres and acres of wildflowers.

In the summer of 1983, my job as a wilderness fire fighter required me to be stationed in a remote village situated on the northern shore of the largest body of water in the interior of Alaska, Lake Minchumina. This lake is located in the geographical center of Alaska. It sits like a jewel in the crown of the Alaska Range, with an imposing view of Denali, the tallest mountain on the North American continent. It was here in this pristine wildflower paradise that I began preparing the Alaskan Flower Essences.

Discovering Flower Essences

My story of the fortunate events that led me to Alaska and to my work of preparing and researching vibrational remedies would not be complete without mentioning how I became aware of flower essences in the first place.

In 1980 I was experiencing various health problems including low-back pain, food allergies, and radical mood swings. I contacted a close friend who was a holistic therapist specializing in vibrational healing. He gave me two Bach remedies and told me to take them for a period of two months. About half way through this dosage cycle I began to notice subtle changes and by the end of it I felt like a different person. However, the most impressive aspect of this initial experience with flower essences was the realization that I had found a new health support system that I would be able to access for the rest of my life.

I was so moved by this experience that I began to search for any information I could find on Dr. Bach's life and work. This search eventually led me to read his book Heal Thyself and to purchase a set of the Bach Flower Remedies. I began to use the remedies on myself, my cats, and my friends, and realized that this was a system of health enhancement that was empowering to the individual. I appreciated the fact that I could pick the essences out for myself and I especially treasured the insight they gave me into the relationship between my mind, emotions, and physical health.

As my understanding and confidence with the Bach Remedies increased, I began to gradually incorporate other systems of flower essences into my personal healing work. I continued to be astounded by their efficacy in dealing with long-standing health problems, some of which I had become resigned to dealing with for the rest of my life. When I began to use the essences on a professional level, I was able to witness similar breakthroughs in others.

It was around this time that I was offered the job of managing the fire station at Lake Minchumina. Little did I know that in this tiny village in the center of Alaska my life's true work would begin.

The Alaskan Flower Essence Project

In the summer of 1983 I was guided to make eight flower essences. This experience led me to the realization that these potent healing energies needed a structured way to move out into the world. I founded the Alaskan Flower Essence Project the following year to coordinate the collection and research of new flower essences from around the state.

My job as a fire fighter in Alaska continued for another eight summers, providing me with many unique opportunities to observe nature and prepare flower and environmental essences in other remote and pristine areas of the state.

Towards the end of this period I began to see that my work with fire was complete and that it was time to devote all of my energies to the essences. This realization led me to retire from my twenty-one year career in fire control in the autumn of 1991 and move the business to Homer, a small coastal town in south central Alaska.

In Homer I was joined in my research and teaching activities by Jane Bell, a flower essence therapist and educator. The scope of our work together expanded in the following summer when Jane and I shared the honor of co-creating the forty-eight Alaskan Gem Elixirs.

Jane and I continue to prepare new flower, gem and environmental essences, but the primary focus of our work together is the ongoing development and presentation of our annual Practitioner Training Program.

I am very grateful for the many opportunities I have had to co-create vibrational essences in this special place called Alaska, and I am honored to be able to share their healing messages with you through this book. May the abundant blessings of nature be with you always.

Steve Johnson
Homer, Alaska
October, 2000

Part One

A Three-Part System of Healing

Introduction

The Birth of a New Consciousness—We are living in one of the most exciting times this planet has ever known. As the energy of change accelerates on the Earth, we are individually and collectively being asked to go through a level of personal transformation never encountered before by the human race.

For many of us, this means witnessing the disintegration of our known reality and experiencing the limbo state that comes before our new reality takes form. It means surrendering the attachments that have kept us tied to the past and allowing whatever remains unresolved in our lives to emerge into the light of truth, wisdom, and understanding.

Contained within the collective shadow of humankind, and within the challenges and lessons that we all face, is our potential for wholeness. While it may seem easier to withdraw from the intensity of what life brings, we must remain true to our inner processes, because it is only from the forge of personal transformation that a new planetary consciousness will be born.

The Law of Dharma—Dharma is defined as the dutiful observance of cosmic law. The Law of Dharma states that we are all spiritual beings who have agreed to come into physical form to fulfill a specific purpose in service to the world. According to this law, each person has a unique talent or gift to offer into this service–no one else has this exact gift or can express it in precisely the same way.

If we are to fulfill our Dharma, we must open to a state of union between our higher and lower selves. We must have alignment and cooperation between our Divine essence or Soul, and our physical body, mind, personality, and ego. We already know how to be spiritual beings without bodies–that is our heritage. Our destiny as third-dimensional beings is to bring all of the power and light of our spiritual selves to the Earth through our physical bodies. The process of achieving this destiny may involve difficult lessons and painful experiences. How we relate to these challenges will determine how successful we are in meeting them.

It is quite common to feel confused, depressed, and overwhelmed in the face of pain and adversity, and to feel victimized by events over which we seem to have no control. As we get caught up the dramas and struggles of life, we lose our perspective. We forget that each lesson that comes is an important part of our divine plan and is here to help us grow stronger.

How do we regain our stability and focus in these times of profound change and transformation? How do we find the strength and awareness to maintain a life orientation that will enable us to complete each life lesson with a minimum of struggle, and emerge with a new part of our Divine Self activated and operating in physical reality?

The Three-Part System of Alaskan Essences—The answers to these questions are all around us. The basic premise of my work is that all aspects of our natural environment, all forms in Nature, embody and generate healing energy. There is an abundance of help and support available, wherever we are, that can ease our learning processes and support the ultimate fulfillment of our life purpose and destiny.

The goal of this book is to reveal, through messages of hope, joy and love, the healing energy that is embodied by this special place called Alaska. The state of Alaska is one of the few areas left on the Earth where the environment is much as it was thousands of years ago. Its extreme climate protects the land from people, but not the people from the elements. Therefore, the plant and elemental kingdoms here are still intact, healthy, and exuberant because much of the state has never been impacted by human activity.

It was this vibrational purity and aliveness that led me to begin preparing essences here from the plant, mineral, and elemental kingdoms. What evolved over the years was an awareness that these three kingdoms possess distinct qualities of vibrational energy that work together to support the entire network of life on our planet. When essences prepared from these three kingdoms are combined therapeutically, they bring to our physical and subtle energy bodies three vital elements that are necessary for a balanced healing process: energy, structure, and conscious awareness. When we have the simultaneous, cooperative action of these three qualities supporting us, we are able to meet our life challenges in a graceful, efficient, and integrated way.

Flower Essences

The gift of the plant kingdom is spiritual consciousness. Flowers are the most evolved part of this kingdom and carry positive, life-affirming patterns of conscious energy. These patterns originate in the higher dimensions and are expressed into our physical world through the specific form of each plant.

Flower essences are a transference of these positive patterns of energy into a liquid medium. This is accomplished by placing healthy flowers at the peak of their blossoming cycle into a bowl of pure water which is potentized by the sun. The resulting mother infusion is then preserved and diluted for internal and external use.

Flower essences catalyze evolution in consciousness. They help us identify emotional and mental qualities within that need to be awakened or strengthened, and stimulate our spiritual growth, which is the ongoing process of grounding our spiritual selves into our physical bodies.

Flower essences are unique in that they are a source of intelligent healing energy that is available to both empower and educate the person taking them. They are empowering because they do not do our healing work for us, but with us—they are powerful catalysts for growth and change but they respect our free will. They are educational because they reveal the causal level of our problems and difficulties. Flower essences illuminate the inner landscape of our psyches and direct our awareness to the conflicting issues and patterns of resistance that are contributing to our dis-ease. They then offer us the precise levels of support we require to resolve our conflicts and release these discordant energies, gently and completely, from our lives. They are like gentle teachers showing us who we really are, and reminding us of our oneness with all life.

These essences may be readily introduced into any life-style or health care program. They do not interfere with, nor are they adversely affected by any other form of treatment, such as homeopathic remedies or prescription drugs. They may be safely used by people of all ages, and can also be a source of healing for the animal and plant kingdoms.

Alaskan Flower Essences

The 72 essences featured in our **Flower Essence Practitioner Kit** were prepared from wild and domestic flowers growing in the state of Alaska. The development of this kit spanned eight years of field work and required thousands of miles of travel throughout the Alaskan wilderness.

The essences contained within this kit represent the primary plant energies occurring in the main bioregions of the state. A bioregion is a geographical area in which the boundaries are determined by nature–by the flora and fauna that live and grow there, and by the landforms and climate that occur there.

The largest bioregion represented in this kit is the vast central interior of Alaska. This area lies between the broad and sweeping expanse of the Brooks Range to the north and the majestic Alaska Range to the south. This territory is also defined topographically by two of the longest rivers flowing through the state, the Yukon and the Koyukuk.

The central interior is known for its extreme seasonal variations in temperature, which can range from -75°F in the winter to 95°F in the summer. The flowering season here starts in deciduous trees such as willow, balsam poplar, birch, and alder before the snow leaves the ground. It continues at a frenetic pace throughout the summer, fueled by sunlight that bathes plants in most areas for up to 20 hours a day.

The plant families in this region are very widespread in their range and dominant in their habitat. This means that there are a relatively small number of plant species, but these occur in huge communities that often extend in unbroken profusion for hundreds of miles. These plants form the vegetative core of the northern or boreal forests of the planet. The essences prepared from them help us transform our core life patterns–those ways of thinking, feeling, and doing that have the most dominant and widespread impact on our lives.

This kit also features essences from plants growing in the extreme northern interior of the state. Most of our essence collection activities in this area were centered around the small village of Bettles, which is situated 35 miles north of the Arctic Circle and only 12 miles south of the Brooks Range. Here the growing season starts in June, after nine months of winter, and seldom lasts longer than 65 days. However, the growth rate of plants in this far northern setting is phenomenal, due to the fact that it never gets dark here from late April to late August. Consequently, these plants express their healing energies in a very intense and directed manner. They encourage us to resolve our issues of trust, self-acceptance, and openness to abundance, so that we can experience the fullness of life in each moment.

A smaller subgroup of essences in this kit were prepared in the Kachemak Bay and Rocky River areas of south central Alaska. This bioregion stretches north and west from the Gulf of Alaska to the Alaska Range and encompasses the northernmost extension of the temperate rain forests on the North American continent.

This area is about 800 miles south of Bettles and exhibits the moderate temperatures, abundant rainfall, and longer growing season characteristic of a maritime climate. Therefore, plants here are able to grow to a much larger size than those in the northern interior. The essences collected from these plants reflect this lush and relaxed atmosphere of growth, helping us strengthen our connection to the Earth, harmonize more fully with our surroundings, and experience peace of mind, even in times of change.

Our **Practitioner Kit** also contains essences from the Rainbow Mountain area of the central Alaskan Range. These essences are unique in that they were prepared in an area surrounded by glaciers, snowfields, and majestic peaks, from plants growing at tree line, or the upper limit of vegetative growth for this latitude. These plants have learned to thrive in some of the most extreme growing conditions found in Alaska by developing unique survival strategies. The adaptive qualities of these plants are embodied by their essences, which help us open to and experience unconditional love and support from inner rather than outer sources, and gain total freedom through healing the past on all levels.

This kit also features a group of essences from plants that are somewhat rare in occurrence and more specialized in their growth patterns. Foremost among these are 12 essences collected from plants with green flowers.

During the process of preparing these green flower essences, we were constantly challenged to open our hearts and perceptions to increasingly subtler levels of physical manifestation. In our attunements we were shown how these essences create pathways of light that can liberate deep levels of pain and tension that are held in the heart–energies that prevent us from coming to a point of true balance within ourselves and, consequently, to a place of genuine contact and partnership with the kingdoms of nature.

The final subset in this kit contains three essences prepared from the flowers of carnivorous plants. These plants possess special qualities of versatility and adaptation that are reflected in the unique ways they have chosen to receive nourishment from their surroundings. The essences made from these plants encourage us to transcend our mental and emotional limitations so that we may know and live the truth of our soul's purpose in this lifetime.

Environmental Characteristics & Flower Essence Qualities

The healing qualities of the Alaskan Flower Essences can be better understood if we consider the following characteristics of the environment in which they were prepared:

Purity: Alaska encompasses an area that is equal to one-fifth of the rest of the United States, but is home to less than 650,000 people. Millions of acres of tundra and forest habitat remain in pristine condition, supporting a variety of plant communities that display a strength, purity, and vitality that is unsurpassed anywhere else in the world.

Contribution: The Alaskan Flower Essences have been collected from plants growing in an environment that is elementally intact. This complete elemental representation facilitates the transference of the healing patterns of the flowers into the essences, allowing them to have the most complete energy structure possible. When we take an essence that has been prepared in these conditions, our body is better able to receive, integrate, and come into alignment with the healing message that is contained within that remedy.

Adaptation: Much of the vegetation in Alaska grows in a thin layer of soil that is underlain by permafrost, or permanently frozen ground. Plants have adjusted to this condition, which limits the amount of nutrients that are usually available in deeper soil, by developing shallow root systems that extend out horizontally from the plant.

In the northern regions of the state the growing season is less than two months long. Many plant species have developed special growth strategies that allow them to flourish during this short growing cycle. These include tough, leathery leaves, strong, woody stems, and the habit of growing close to the ground in mats so that they will be more protected from the wind. Some plants even possess the ability to keep growing after the first killing frost, and survive in temperatures down to 28°F.

Contribution: The dictionary defines the word adaptation as, "an alteration or adjustment in structure or habits, often hereditary, by which a species or individual improves its condition in relationship to its environment". Plants growing in Alaska have evolved for many eons in very harsh conditions, proving that it is possible to adapt to and prosper in an environment that seems to be more challenging than supportive.

The essences prepared from these plants help us refine our understanding of what support really is and teach us how to open ourselves to it unconditionally. We are then better able to respond to our challenges and use them as opportunities to transform our attitudes about struggle, conflict, and difficulty.

The Energy of Transformation: The nature of Alaska is expressed through the constant movement of unbridled energy. This movement is most obviously expressed by the rapidly changing weather and by the pace at which all things grow during the intense summers of perpetual light. There is a constant pressure here to move, to act, and to transform the old into the new.

Contribution: The Alaskan Flower Essences are awakeners and catalysts for dynamic change. They help us become aware of the lessons and shifts in consciousness that are required by the life path we have chosen to follow, and help us move through these in a focused and graceful way. They also provide support for those who have chosen to do their inner work at an accelerated pace, and for those who are in the midst of a major transition and need additional support to complete it.

Connection to the Cosmos: While a few species have enjoyed a history of traditional use by the native populations of Alaska, most of the plants growing here have not had much direct interaction with humans on an ongoing basis. Rather, their main association has been with the other kingdoms of nature and with the cosmos.

Contribution: These plants embody a very direct connection between the Earth and the spiritual realms. Their essences are especially helpful in grounding those people who have agreed to be of service to humanity, but who are attempting to fulfill this agreement from an ungrounded or disembodied place.

These essences can also help us open our awareness to spirit as it is expressed through nature, by teaching us how to deepen our attunement to the animal, plant, and mineral kingdoms.

The lack of past association with the human kingdom also means that some of these plants have embodied their vibrational healing qualities very recently. Therefore the essences prepared from these plants are particularly relevant to the challenges we are currently facing.

Environmental Essences

The gift of the environment is sustenance. The environment sustains our lives in all ways, providing the physical and energetic nourishment we need to maintain our bodies and continue the evolution of our species.

The environment is a unique collection of elements, just as we are. In fact, we and the environment, at our most basic levels, have the same elemental composition and are constantly sharing these elements with one another.

The preparation of an environmental essence begins with the identification of specific elemental qualities in the environment. We then enter into a co-creative healing agreement by extending an attunement from our hearts to the devic and elemental beings that represent these qualities.

Through this attunement we communicate our love and blessings, and ask that the energies we have identified be transferred into the bowl of water that we have prepared. We accept the essence gratefully as the environment responds. The resulting essence is totally unique, as the vibrational qualities it contains can never be duplicated in exactly the same way.

The healing concept behind the co-creation of environmental essences is that through our focused intent and with the cooperation of nature we are able to access and make use of the powerful elemental forces of the environment to bring about change and transformation at very deep levels of our beings.

Environmental essences are very catalytic in their actions and are often indicated when a strong cleansing energy is needed to bring vitality to someone who is not responding to other therapies or modalities. They provide a strong base of support for our work with flower essences, lending energy and vitality to the healing processes catalyzed by the flowers. These essences from the environment also help us create clear and balanced inner environments which can support positive change and growth. This is especially important for people who live within a toxic or abusive family dynamic.

The Alaskan Environmental essences are extremely effective tools for Space Clearing. This process involves cleansing and releasing old energies from our living and working environments and then recharging and revitalizing these spaces with the fresh, clean energy of nature.

Space Clearing with environmental essences is particularly beneficial for those living in crowded and polluted urban areas where the natural elemental forces have been weakened or dissipated all together. These essences can also provide balance and stability in emergency situations such as natural disasters when the environment itself is in transition.

Alaskan Environmental Essences

I was inspired to begin a collection of environmental essences in 1984 by an experience with a very special storm cloud whose powerful presence led to the preparation of the Solstice Storm essence. The experience of co-creating this essence opened my awareness to the vast healing power contained within the myriad expressions of air, earth, fire, and water that are found in nature.

The subsequent development of this collection came about in two ways. Some of the essences were prepared in response to a natural, spontaneous event in nature, such as the Northern Lights. Others required travel to certain parts of the state in order to capture the energetic expressions of more permanent features of the Alaskan environment, such as Portage Glacier.

I was eventually guided to incorporate essences from special locations outside the state of Alaska, and this resulted in the addition of the Polar Ice essence, which was prepared near the North Pole; Chalice Well, from the Chalice Well Gardens of Glastonbury, England; Greenland Icecap, which was collected on the island of Greenland; and Liard Hot Springs, from the province of British Columbia, Canada.

Gem Elixirs

The gifts of the mineral kingdom are structure and stability. Each mineral on our Earth is a stable structure that helps anchor the energies of consciousness into form.

Gem elixirs are liquid preparations that contain the potentized vibrations of the mineral kingdom. They are made by placing a mineral specimen in a bowl of pure water that is then activated by the energy of the sun. This water receives the energy imprint of the mineral used, and is then preserved and diluted for internal and external use.

The primary action of gem elixirs is to stabilize and balance the energy field. This includes the subtle bodies which make up the aura, and the chakras, or main energy centers of the body. Gem elixirs work by catalyzing the release of stress and tension that has accumulated in the auric field. As these dissonant energies are released, the subtle bodies and chakras come back into alignment, and the physical body is able to regain its natural state of balance, stability, and resistance to stress.

Gem elixirs provide us with the means to transform the vibrational structure of the physical body so that it can stay in harmony with our consciousness as it grows and expands within the body. This is especially relevant for those involved in flower essence therapy.

Soul growth that is catalyzed through the use of flower essences steps up or accelerates the frequency of consciousness inhabiting the body. If we do not match this rapid expansion of consciousness with a corresponding change in the frequency of the physical body itself, we will not be able to maintain this growth in a balanced way.

This kind of imbalance is currently quite common, as many people who are striving to become more spiritual and attuned to the "light" are at the same time ignoring the needs of their bodies. We cannot grow and expand spiritually from a structural foundation that is poorly built or inadequately maintained. Sooner or later, we will overextend the physical body's capacity to integrate change, and it will respond by getting sick. We will then need to go through a period of rest and reevaluation.

Gem elixirs address this situation by working with us to adjust and realign the energetic structure of our bodies at the molecular level. These adjustments make it possible for us to maintain the stability of our physical forms while increasing our capacity to experience transformational growth in consciousness.

Alaskan Gem Elixirs

The Alaskan Gem Elixirs were co-created by Jane Bell and Steve Johnson in 1992. Our intention was to prepare a collection of remedies that would blend the healing energies of the mineral kingdom with the strength and purity of the Alaskan environment.

Historically speaking, much of the information that has been collected on the healing qualities of a given gemstone is derived from its physical signature. This signature would include the crystal system or family the mineral belongs to, its color, hardness, and chemical composition, and the geologic process by which it was formed. In addition, our research focused on the subtle invisible geometry or energy pattern of the stone, which is held at the devic level of the mineral kingdom and by the elemental forces that were called into service during the preparation process.

Each Alaskan Gem Elixir was co-created in a unique wilderness setting chosen for the particular elemental qualities it embodied, qualities that would most effectively anchor the healing pattern of the stone into the water. For example, a few of these elixirs were prepared next to a glacier, some on the shore of one of the largest lakes in the state, located 150 miles from the nearest highway, and several in a high meadow filled with wild flowers and surrounded by peaks of the Alaska Range, including Denali, the tallest mountain in North America.

Chakra and Subtle Body Anatomy

If we are to gain a full appreciation for the healing potential of vibrational essences, we must also have an understanding of our nonphysical, or subtle, anatomy. There are currently many systems of thought used to explain the structure and function of the human aura. I have used the following system in conjunction with gem elixirs and flower essences for many years. I encourage you to adapt this information to your own understanding where necessary.

The human aura consists of several layers of interpenetrating energy fields called subtle bodies which surround each other and the physical body in a series of concentric circles. In addition, there are seven chakras, or dynamic energy centers, which also interpenetrate the physical body and are located from the base of the spine to the top of the head. Each chakra vibrates at a higher frequency than the one below it, and each subtle body vibrates at a higher frequency than the one it surrounds. Chronic problems in the physical body may often be the result of imbalances which originate in one or more of the subtle bodies or chakras.

The Subtle Bodies

Etheric Body—The closest subtle body to the physical is the etheric. The etheric body hugs the physical body like a second skin and is the interface between it and the rest of the subtle energy system. The etheric body has an active relationship to all of the chakras.

The importance of having a clear etheric body is that blockages here can impede the two-way flow of energy and information between the physical body and the universal field. This can result in a buildup of toxins in the physical and etheric bodies, and a corresponding lack of physical vitality.

Emotional Body—This subtle body, which is also referred to as the astral body, is the connecting medium between the mental and physical bodies and is the seat of all emotional experience.

Emotions are patterns of organized energy designed to carry out specific actions. These patterns are set into motion by thought and intent. Emotions have natural life cycles that normally lead to their own energetic resolution, however, suppression, manipulation, and resistance often prevent these cycles from completing themselves.

Once an emotion has been suppressed, it needs to be reactivated so its energy can move again toward completion. It is through constant activation and integration of our emotional energy that we are able to carry out our intentions without tension building up in our emotional and physical bodies.

Mental Body—The mental body is our connection to the mental plane and the energies of universal mind, and is the repository of our own personal thought forms and belief systems. This subtle energy field is also the connecting link between the emotional body and the spiritual body.

A healthy and balanced relationship between the mental and emotional bodies is absolutely necessary, as it is the mental body that gives the energies of the emotional body focus and direction. Injuries or tears in the boundary between the mental and emotional bodies can account for many of the symptoms that are currently referred to as mental illness.

Spiritual Body—Sometimes referred to as the causal body, this energy field is the most subtle of all. It interpenetrates the mental body and forms the boundary between who we are and the universal field of All That Is. It is through the spiritual body that we receive nurturing from the spiritual dimensions of energy and consciousness. It is here that these energies are transmuted, or their frequencies lowered, so that they can be used by the rest of our energy system.

The Chakras

The chakras are energy centers for the development and embodiment of different levels of human awareness and experience. Together they form an intricate system of transformers—each chakra is capable of changing the vibratory rate of the energy that flows through it.

All seven chakras vibrate at a different frequency and therefore each is associated with a different color. The following chart illustrates the relationship between the colors of the stones used to prepare our collection of gem elixirs and the chakras they correspond to:

Black, Grey, Red—1st Chakra
Orange, Brown—2nd Chakra
Gold, Yellow—3rd Chakra
Green, Pink—4th Chakra
Blue—5th Chakra
Lavender, Indigo—6th Chakra
Violet, Purple—7th Chakra
Clear, Multicolored—All Chakras

First Chakra—The Base Chakra is located near the base of the spine for men and between the ovaries for women. It is the center of one's physical relationship to the Earth and is concerned with issues and activities pertinent to survival, such as security, sustenance, and shelter. Blockages in this chakra translate as an inability to fully connect one's spiritual energy to the physical dimension. A strong and clear first chakra indicates that an individual has dealt successfully with his or her basic survival needs, has a strong grounding connection with the Earth, and is free to concentrate on the development of the higher chakras.

Second Chakra—This chakra is also called the Sexual or Splenic Chakra. This energy vortex is located approximately three fingers below the navel. It is the center of creativity and of deep feeling, or sympathetic resonance, with other beings. Many of the so-called negative emotions, including fear, jealousy, rage, and anger are associated with this chakra, as well as a person's ability to feel what another person is feeling. Blockages here can influence how a person relates sexually and emotionally to others, as well as how they relate to or communicate with their own feelings.

Third Chakra—This is the Solar Plexus Chakra. It is located directly beneath the sternum and is concerned with the development of identity, ego, personality, and the right use of power. The third chakra is our energy distribution system. Its job, technically speaking, is to collect energy and send it where it is needed in the body. This is also the center that is connected to out-of-the-body experiences such as dreams and astral travel.

A correctly functioning third chakra does not collect energy from outside sources, but rather from within, tapping into inexhaustible universal sources that are available to us all. People with dysfunctional third chakras will, on the other hand, attempt to get energy from other people, places, and things in inappropriate ways. Such persons may suffer from low self-esteem and have unresolved issues concerning the abuse of control and power, and consequently will have difficulty taking responsibility for their own actions.

Fourth Chakra—This center is called the Heart Chakra. It is located halfway between the sternum and the throat. The heart chakra is the primary point of connection between our higher selves and the Earth. It is also the focal point in the physical body where the energies and activities of the three lower and the three higher chakras can come together in unity and harmony. With an open and fully functioning heart chakra we can infuse our needs for security, connection, creativity, and power with the benevolent virtues of trust, affinity, love, and compassion. A strong and clear heart chakra is also vital to the balanced development of the higher chakras and the abilities associated with them.

The heart is also where we store our deepest pain, sorrow, and trauma. Much of our initial work with this chakra, therefore, is with the release of these energies, so that the forces of love can penetrate and completely infuse our lives.

Fifth Chakra—This is the Throat Chakra. It is the center of higher communication, where we develop clairaudience, or the ability to hear our own inner voice, and to be in telepathic contact with other beings, with or without bodies.

The fifth chakra is also where we develop pragmatic intuition and the ability to express ourselves verbally. Blockages in this chakra usually manifest physically as problems with the ears, teeth, jaw, and throat, as well as difficulties with hearing, speaking, and processing information.

Sixth Chakra—This energy center is also called the Third Eye or Brow Chakra. It is located in the center of the forehead and is associated with higher perception and seeing. It is here that we develop clairvoyance–the ability to perceive that which is vibrating at a higher frequency than the physical. It is also where we develop abstract intuition-the ability to arrive at a conclusion without a logical progression of thoughts.

When this chakra is underdeveloped, a person has difficulty seeing what is in their highest good or sensing the truth of a situation. When this center is too open and undisciplined, it can lead a person to live more in their visions than in their physical body.

Seventh Chakra—This energy center is also called the Crown Chakra and is located at the top of the head. This chakra is our point of connection to the universal, nonphysical aspects of self–also called the Higher Self or Oversoul. It is also the center of unitive consciousness, of knowingness–the ability to be still and know.

With this chakra, we are primarily concerned with development, rather than with the release of blockages. However, it is important that this chakra be open, clear, and connected to all the lower chakras so that universal life force energy will be able to flow completely through the individual and into the Earth.

Part Two

Essence Application
and Use

Seven Levels of Application

The Alaskan Flower, Gem, and Environmental essences can be used on seven distinct levels to bring support, awareness and healing energy to our human family.

While there is a certain logic to the way these levels are presented in this book, there is no set order to how they should be approached. The intent of this information is to suggest a broader framework of application for the essences, not to dictate a certain sequence in which they should be used. Indeed, our approach to this work should be based on inner timing and how these different levels manifest in the course of our lives.

(Appendix C, on page 277, features a chart of the twelve Alaskan essences that are the most applicable to each of the seven levels given here.)

1) Getting Here—Nature provides qualities of energy and support that are absolutely essential to the maintenance of physical health and to the manifestation of life purpose. Our ability to access this support is determined by the strength and depth of our energetic connection to the Earth and by the quality of our heart connection with nature.

When our physical bodies are firmly grounded to the planet and our hearts are open to the heart of nature, we are in position to access the unlimited energetic support that is available from this and other dimensions of consciousness. As we allow ourselves to become more open and connected, we are able to maintain higher levels of health and life energy and thus offer greater levels of service to our families and to the planet. We are like trees sinking long roots into the ground to draw on deep reserves of water and nutrients so we can grow and share our beauty with others.

The process of getting here is called incarnation. This process does not stop when we are born, but continues until we lay our bodies to their final rest. This is because as humans we have chosen to incarnate through the learning of life lessons (karma) and through helping others learn their life lessons (dharma).

When our learning experiences take on a high level of intensity or when we are challenged on our path of service, a common tendency is to retreat into that realm where most of us feel more comfortable, the spiritual plane. This is where we came from, it is our true home, and most, if not all of us, long to return there. In truth, the only way for us to go home is to anchor the reality of the spiritual plane into this dimension through our physical bodies.

Once we accept this orientation, we begin to understand that the challenges and difficulties we encounter in life are all opportunities to strengthen our connection to spirit from within the physical body. We also begin to see that to be truly present in this world we must have the willingness to be with any unresolved emotions, such as fear and grief, that may have previously caused us to have a conditional acceptance of our physical bodies.

Again, the tendency is to disassociate from these pockets of energy and reside in those parts of ourselves that we feel more comfortable with. This is like trying to live in two bodies at the same time. It takes a tremendous amount of energy to maintain this split and the tension created by it will often manifest as confusion, lack of focus, low vitality, and over-sensitivity to others and to the environment.

Vibrational essences are very important at this level of application. They help us become aware of, be present with, and ultimately release the resistance we have to embodying our spiritual selves in physical form. With this quality of support from nature, we can use each life experience to become more focused, unified, and secure in our bodies and on the planet.

2) Emotional Awareness and Healing—As we become more present in our bodies, we also become more aware of our emotions. If our estrangement from the physical body has been lengthy or extreme, chances are we will have a backlog of unfinished emotional business to attend to. This backlog will consist of emotional experiences from this and other lifetimes that have not yet come to completion because they have been deactivated or frozen.

An emotional experience becomes frozen when we do not feel safe or supported enough to express strong feelings such as anger or rage when it is entirely appropriate to do so. Instead, these feelings are suppressed and eventually covered over with other emotions such as shame, guilt, or sadness.

The process of moving through these layers of built-up emotional energy is called peeling. Flower essences are particularly useful for this kind of emotional integration. Initially, they can help us become aware of the fact that we have an emotional blockage. Then they will work with us to discharge it, layer by layer, until we get down to our core emotions and the lessons connected with them. Finally, they will help us integrate these lessons and weave their positive qualities into the fabric of our lives.

3) Physical Awareness and Release—Some people may require an additional level of support from nature to completely release certain levels of blocked emotional energy from their physical bodies. This is especially true with powerful emotions such as anger or rage that are connected to experiences of abuse.

Individuals who have been abused often build up a tremendous amount of physical and emotional tension called armoring. This armoring serves to insulate them somewhat from their pain and trauma but it also holds these energies in place. In such cases, several courses of essences may be needed to help these individuals become aware of the fact that they have this armoring. Additional essences can then be selected to facilitate its gradual release.

Subsequent essences may also be indicated to help with the forgiveness process. This work must be completed before an individual will be able to totally release the effects of the traumatic experience from the energetic structure of the body.

At each step in this process, vibrational essences can provide us with the means to exchange the physical, emotional, and mental pain and trauma that is present in our bodies for the fresh, clean, and alive energies of nature. In this way, we become renewed at the deepest levels of our beings.

4) Healing the Heart/Attunement With Nature—One of the highest functions of the heart chakra is to receive unconditional love and make this energy available for all healing work that needs to be done in the body. However, the heart is also where we hold our deepest fears and traumas. These patterns of tension can block or severely limit the circulation of love in the heart, and consequently limit the flow of healing energy in the body.

The process of healing the heart with vibrational essences is cyclical. As each layer of fear or pain is contacted and held in unconditional love, corresponding layers of tension are released, and we are able to open to stronger currents of life energy. This strengthening of the heart forces enables us to address and heal deeper levels of fear and pain, which in turn allows a greater flow of life force energy to circulate throughout the heart and body.

As we begin to release all that is not love from our hearts, we also begin to dissolve the illusion of separation. We began to create this illusion eons ago to protect ourselves from those aspects of life and nature that we feared or did not understand. I believe we are at a point in our planetary evolution where separation is more a limitation than a source of security. In fact, our true happiness and security on this planet is now largely dependent upon our ability to completely dissolve this veil of separation. We must learn again how to live in harmony with nature and all other living beings, and to do this we must first remember how to communicate with them.

The heart is our primary point of connection to all life on Earth. Vibrational essences can help us release the deep levels of pain and tension that have occupied our hearts, enabling us to see more clearly into nature and connect energetically with the hearts of others. This attunement, or empathic communication, is a skill we are all born with, but it must be awakened and refined if we are to realize our divine potential as co-creators on this planet.

5) Relationships and Karma—One of the most important and empowering contributions we can make in this area is to accept responsibility for what we have created in our lives. Practicing this act on a regular basis makes it possible for us to live each day with awareness and understanding, rather than with the feeling of being constantly tossed about by events and experiences beyond our control.

Essences can help us become aware of the past agreements and contracts we have made with the members of our soul family, enabling us to better understand and take responsibility for the reality of our present experience, especially with regard to the primary relationships we are involved in.

Vibrational essences can also empower us to avoid creating negative karma for the future by helping us make better choices and decisions in the present. They can help us to see our true intentions and motivations for wanting to be involved in a relationship, and also teach us how to attract relationships that are in alignment with who we really are.

Essences can also help us identify emotional and mental patterns that have been carried over from one or more previous lifetimes. These can often be identified by their impact on certain parts of the physical body, which we may injure repeatedly, or by a chronic illness that defies standard medical diagnosis.

6) Awareness and Activation of Life Purpose—This area of inner work is tremendously important and its relevance to all other aspects of an individual's health and well-being should not be underestimated.

There are three key stages in the process of activating life purpose. The initial step is to become aware of our true nature–who we are at our most essential level. A conscious and committed program of flower essence therapy is one of the most effective ways of achieving this awareness of true self.

The next step is to access the content of the service agreements or contracts we entered into before coming here. We may need additional essences to help us release blockages on the mental and emotional levels so this information will be consciously available to us.

The third, and often most difficult step, is to translate this new awareness of life purpose into practical action on the physical plane. We may find that in order to follow our true purpose we will need to change careers, our place of residence, our group of friends, and even our life-style. These actions require a tremendous amount of courage and faith because they ask us to let go of our current network of support. Vibrational essences are especially important during these times of transition because they can help us connect to new sources of support that will balance and stabilize us as we make these important and necessary adjustments to the structure of our lives.

We need to be able to receive nurturing from all areas of our lives, but especially from the work we have chosen to do. The process of becoming aligned with life purpose brings us into a flow of energy that we can then access to carry out this purpose. This energy flow will be increasingly available to us as we deepen our commitment to do our service from a place of giving, rather than from a place of selfishness and personal gain. As we learn to give truthfully from the heart, without attachment, we will receive all that we need.

7) Spiritual Growth and Awareness—The first six levels of essence application are concerned primarily with healing the past so that we are free to live more fully in the present. The seventh level is concerned with expanding our awareness of and connection to spiritual dimensions of consciousness. The essences in this category have a wide range of application that is not so much determined by where we are on our spiritual path, as by our willingness to receive spiritual support, directly and in the moment.

There is an unlimited amount of spiritual support available to us, but we have to open the door and invite it in. We always have a choice. We can continue to struggle and perhaps create a crisis or get sick in order to feel supported. Or we can open our minds and hearts to the benevolent energies of the higher dimensions that are constantly present within us and all around us.

The first choice requires hard work. The second requires us to suspend all effort and just receive. With the help of the essences, we can drop our old habits of struggle and learn to consciously and gratefully accept the spiritual support that is offered to each and every one of us, unconditionally.

Essence Application and Use

Choosing Essences

There are many techniques and methods currently being used to select essences. These range from the more intuitive techniques of pendulum analysis, placing one's hands over the essence bottles, and kinesiology, to more rational approaches, such as reading a repertory or an essence selection guide and using the interview process. The most important consideration here is not which technique to use, but the degree of confidence and clarity we develop with the one we choose.

Our ability to select essences will mature as we learn more about the essences and about ourselves. The main issue that surfaces for people who are beginning to develop their testing skills is whether they trust their ability to connect with accurate sources of information. If we are to establish a high level of trust in this area, we must allow ourselves to make choices and then act on them. We will always be given feedback on our level of accuracy. From this we will be able to make the necessary adjustments to facilitate deeper contact with our own information or with the soul of another being. All that is really necessary is an open heart, a flexible mind, a willingness to learn, and a commitment to practice.

The value of any selection method or approach will also be determined by the clarity and focus of our intention and by our ability to ask good questions. The process of asking a good question begins with taking time to consider what it is we really want to know. Once we have established a clear intention, we can make a statement of it and repeat this to ourselves or to the client we are working with. It is also helpful to prioritize our inquiries and ask the most important questions first. Begin with questions that can be answered with a simple yes or no, and just ask one question at a time.

Internal Use

There are two categories of use for essences that are to be taken internally. The first one can be called situational and may include the short-term use of certain essences during a personal emergency or for immediate support during a transformational process. For this type of application we recommend that our flower, gem, and environmental essences, and especially our combination formulas, be used at their existing or stock level of dilution. Drops may be taken directly from the stock bottle or added to a small amount of liquid and sipped at regular intervals during the day.

The primary use of essences that are to be taken internally is referred to as long term, where the intent is to gently transform core issues and gradually liberate patterns of behavior that are no longer useful or appropriate. An extended period of time during which a particular group of essences should be taken is called a dosage cycle. The average length of a dosage cycle is 30 to 40 days, and for this, one would need to make up two or three dosage bottles. These can be prepared according to the following instructions.

Preparing Dosage Bottles—First choose the appropriate essences. Then fill a clean 1 oz. (30 ml) glass dropper bottle with pure or distilled water and add two drops of each selected essence. A preservative, such as a good quality brandy or cognac, is recommended to preserve the clarity and stability of the solution. The amount will vary depending on how warm a climate you live in, but a good rule of thumb is 25% of the volume of the bottle. Those with a sensitivity to alcohol may want to use an equal amount of apple cider vinegar or vegetable glycerin as a substitute for the brandy.

The standard adult dosage from this level of dilution is four drops, four times a day, but individual testing is the best way to arrive at the correct dosage amount and frequency. Small children and animals will usually need to take the essences less frequently than adults.

Please note that the frequency, or the number of times the essences are taken, not the amount taken, increases the strength of their effect.

External Use

The external use of essences can be quite effective when there are circumstances that prohibit oral administration, or when external methods offer benefits that cannot be practically achieved otherwise. The primary methods of external application are broadcasting, which is the introduction of essences into a designated space using a carrier such as water, and the direct or topical application of essences to certain parts of the body, by themselves or mixed into creams, salves, or oils.

Environmental Cleansing—All of the Alaskan essences can be used externally to cleanse, balance, and uplift one's home or work environment. For example, you may want to purify the energy of the bedroom where someone is recuperating from an illness, or clear the kitchen after a family argument.

In the workplace, essences can be used to help you create a more focused and creative work environment, or to clear the air after a staff meeting. Professional therapists can select essences to facilitate the kind of healing work they are doing and to cleanse and recycle the energy in their treatment rooms.

Regardless of the application, you will first need to do a consultation for the room or area you are working with. The purpose of this is to identify what kind of energy you want to bring into your space. Do you want essences that cleanse and release, are uplifting and joyful, or nurturing and soothing? Once you have made your selections, the essences can be introduced or broadcast into the space in a variety of ways.

• Add several drops of each essence to a bowl of water and place it in a special space in your home.

• Add drops to a humidifier, air conditioner, or air purification system.

• Fountains are very popular in Feng Shui for circulating chi or life force in the home or office. Essences can be placed in a fountain each day to bring certain vibrational qualities to the surrounding area.

• Make up a misting bottle. Misting bottles are portable vibrational air fresheners. They also make great traveling companions–use them on the airplane and to freshen your hotel room upon arrival.

Preparing Misting Bottles—You will first need a bottle that will accept a spray attachment. Add two to four drops of each selected essence, along with drops of any essential oils you wish to use, and fill the bottle with water. A small amount of alcohol may be added as a preservative. Separate bottles can be made up for home and office and these areas can be misted as often as you like.

Topical Application

Bath Therapy—This is a very effective way to use essences topically, whether you are at home or traveling. Simply prepare your bath water as hot as is comfortable, add two to four drops of each selected essence, and relax! Using gem elixirs and environmental essences in the bath after flying is a very effective way to recover from fatigue and jet lag, or the disorientation that comes from crossing many time zones in a day. Baths are also a great way to administer essences to young children.

Energy Balancing/Reiki—All the Alaskan essences can be used in conjunction with many hands-on healing techniques to help balance and stabilize a person's subtle energy system. The therapist giving the treatment will first want to determine which essences are needed and where they are needed. Appropriate areas of the body can then be anointed with drops of selected flower, gem, or environmental essences. Reiki or similar radiant healing energies can then be directed through these areas to enhance the balancing process.

Massage and Bodywork—Essences can also be used to facilitate the movement of energy during any kind of massage or bodywork session. The body holds on to any trauma it has experienced until it receives the encouragement and support it needs to release it. Using essences in massage formulas facilitates this releasing process. The therapist may add a few drops of each selected essence to the massage oil or rub drops between his or her hands before and during the session.

Self-Care—Adding essences to face creams, moisturizers, lotions, and other personal care products will enhance their nurturing properties and facilitate the healing of old and new injuries, skin problems, and areas of the body that are recovering from trauma.

Household Maintenance—essences can be added to all cleaning products used in the house, and to the washing machine. You can also add essences to house paint to set a certain energy in the room you are painting.

Using Essences with the Animal Kingdom

Establishing a Healing Relationship

In our work with animals I feel there are two main considerations to be addressed. The first one is: on what basis do we establish our healing relationship with the animal kingdom? In other words, how can those of us who are concerned for the health and well-being of our animal companions best communicate our concern and truly be of service to them?

I believe that a healing relationship between the animal and human kingdoms must be a co-creative one, and an important first step in the establishment of any co-creative relationship is to examine our perceptions. In this instance, how do we perceive the animals in our lives? Do we see them as beasts of burden, as pets, or do we see them as noble companions and recognize that they have their own rich soul lives, high intelligence, and evolutionary paths?

Another important key to this healing relationship is our willingness to let the animals be our teachers. If we approach this work with open hearts and minds we will be able to receive many valuable insights as to what is really taking place on the soul level within the animal kingdom. This deeper understanding will help us extend our love and concern in ways that will truly contribute to their health and well-being.

My second area of consideration can be summed up by these two questions, Why do animals get sick, and what level of care should we provide for them when they do?

In my essence consultations, I have not seen one case where emotional blockages were not a major contributing factor to the symptoms or behavior presented by the animal. Animals live very much in the emotional realm. They have well-developed emotional bodies and are highly skilled at absorbing and reflecting emotional energy. In fact, part of their soul agreement with the human kingdom is to help us work with and balance our own emotional energies.

Difficulties can begin when an animal takes in more emotional energy than it is capable of processing or reflecting back. Eventually, physical symptoms can manifest that will be quite similar to those found in humans who are also dealing with emotional blockages.

Sadly, one of the main sources of emotional distress in animals is abuse, and it is regrettable that most of the abuse suffered by animals comes from humans, either through direct and sometimes violent physical contact or by passive neglect.

Many of our so-called domesticated animals have been deeply traumatized by a lack of emotional care and nurturing, and in severe cases, by an absence of the most basic physical necessities such as food and water. This kind of neglect can leave scars that, while not necessarily visible, can seriously affect an animal's behavior and sense of well-being for the rest of its life. This is a very important point to remember when working with stray dogs and cats, as it is difficult to know exactly what sorts of experiences these animals encountered before they arrived in your care.

When our animals get sick, I believe our primary responsibility as guardians is to provide them with a level of care that is oriented towards discovering and treating the root causes of their behavioral problems and illnesses. It follows that any animal health care plan should include holistic therapies that are capable of addressing imbalances at the emotional level.

Vibrational essences are especially well suited for this task and can be easily integrated into any program of care, as they do not interfere with, nor are they adversely affected by other forms of treatment, such as homeopathic remedies or prescription drugs. However, essences will be most effective when the animal is receiving proper exercise and nutrition, abundant emotional nurturing, appropriate medical attention and, of course, lots of love.

Application Guidelines

There are two distinct levels of consciousness and evolution in the animal kingdom—the group soul level and the individuated level. All animals can be approached on the group soul level, and those who have developed more independent or individualized personalities can be approached at the level of their development.

Wild animals generally maintain good health except when their habitat is threatened by natural forces or partially destroyed by a human caused catastrophe, such as the Exxon Valdez oil spill in the Prince William Sound of Alaska. In these kinds of situations, essences can be used where appropriate to help heal the shock and trauma of the affected animals. Wild animals who have been captured, sold, and eventually rescued, can be treated for the shock of being taken away from their natural environment and separated from their families and mates. In many cases, they will completely recover and can be released again into the wild, or into protected areas.

Domestic farm animals, such as horses, cows, and sheep, have developed varying degrees of individuation as a result of their history of close association with humans. Therefore, we can treat individual farm animals that are exhibiting health problems and also use essences to support the health of an entire herd or family group.

The possibilities for using essences with highly individualized animals such as dogs and cats are almost as varied and numerous as those available to humans. One must realize, however, that even though these animals have reached a high degree of soul individuation, they are still very dependent upon the emotional bond they share with the humans and animals they live with.

The energy dynamic of a typical family with one or more animals in residence can be broken down into three distinct levels. Each one of these may need to be addressed during the course of treatment. At the first level we find issues that belong only to the animal and are not shared by any other member of the family. On the second level there will be shared lessons or opportunities for growth that the animal and one or more family members (animal or human) have in common. And on the third level we will often find a situation where the health of an animal is being severely impacted by the actions of other humans or animals living within the family dynamic. It is this third level that often presents the greatest challenge, because everyone involved will need to become aware of and take responsibility for their impact before the situation can be fully resolved.

It follows that if we want the animals in our care to derive the greatest possible benefit from the essences they are taking, we must be willing to grow and change with them. Otherwise, we will only be confusing an animal by giving it a catalyst to grow, and then blocking the potential of that growth with our own resistance. The best scenario is when all members of the family, human and otherwise, are using essences. This approach allows common issues to emerge and heal in a much more cohesive way—one that will be easier and more graceful for all involved.

It is not uncommon to be blind to some of the issues affecting your animals, especially if these issues are part of your own growth process. If you are periodically unable to get a clear sense of what essences your animal companions need, it might be advantageous to have a qualified practitioner or holistic veterinarian assist you in the selection process.

A Day in the Life

There are certain times in the life of an animal, and during the course of events in the average household, when essences can be particularly beneficial.

The first one is the birth of any family member, animal or human. This auspicious occasion is usually accompanied by an abundance of excitement, stress, confusion, and scattered energy, and essences can bring much needed qualities of awareness, grounding, and balance to the situation.

Illness and disease often require an extended or long-term application of vibrational essences. For chronic illness, essences should be administered in consecutive dosage cycles given over the course of several months or longer depending on the life history of the animal. Animals have very well-developed and complex emotional lives and will often exhibit a layering of issues that must be approached one at a time on a priority basis.

Injuries to an animal demand a more immediate and short-term application of essences, as well as other appropriate forms of medical care. Once the immediate injury has been taken care of, please remember to treat all other members of the family for shock. Most animals are particularly sensitive to the fact that one of their kind has been hurt, and many will try to absorb some of the energy of the situation.

With serious injuries, we will often be challenged to make a decision whether to involve an animal in heroic medical intervention to prolong its life. Essences can help us tune into, understand, and respect the soul timing of the injured one and the process it is going through. If it is indeed time for that animal to make its transition, then we need to be able to facilitate that process.

Essences are also very important to use during the death of an animal who is passing on due to old age or natural causes. They can provide a much needed level of support for the journey the animal is about to take, and also help those family members who are involved to see the death process as one of joyous release and transformation.

An unfortunate but all too common occurrence in our modern world is divorce. The breakup of a family usually requires some members to move and find a different place to live, and this can be as emotionally traumatic to an animal as it is to the children and parents. In this instance, essences can be used to help an animal regain its sense of equilibrium as the family dynamic is restructured.

Another difficult situation can arise when a family goes on vacation and the animals are left at home, sometimes with a house-sitter who is a stranger to them. Essences can be selected which will help the animals adjust to the shift in energy that will occur when their humans leave and to help them get used to having a different person in the house taking care of them. These essences should be given for several days before the family members leave, during their entire absence, and for a few days after they return.

Travel is also stressful for some animals, especially air travel. A custom mix of essences can be selected and added to the water that will be available to the them during the flight to help with the stresses of confinement, noise, and turbulence.

There are several Alaskan essences that have proven helpful in many of the situations mentioned in this section. Please refer to the **Animals/Animal Care** heading in Part Seven of this book for more information.

Oral Administration—Dosage bottles for animals are prepared in the same way they are for humans. I recommend, however, that you use glycerine instead of brandy for the preservative.

If an animal is healthy enough, it will establish its own frequency of taking essences. In most cases, you will only need to add two drops from the dosage bottle to the watering container each time it is filled up. An exception to this is when you are treating an acute or emergency condition or when the animal is not able to drink regularly. In these situations, give the essences directly to the animal as often as necessary, placing the drops inside the mouth if possible.

Generally speaking, essence dosage cycles for animals will be of a shorter duration than they are for most humans. This is because animals usually demonstrate the positive effects of essences more quickly than people, with the exception of young children. I believe this is because they have not created separation from the other kingdoms of nature, and they do not compartmentalize their life experiences as humans do.

External Application—This is a very effective method of application for animals who are unable to take their essences orally, and for those who are suffering from external injuries. Essences may be added to a misting bottle and sprayed around or directly on the animal or, if appropriate, added to a salve and rubbed into the coat and skin.

Using Essences With the Plant Kingdom

Essences and Gardening

In light of our concerns for the health and well-being of our gardens there are many situations where we might want to use essences. I will list them here in a loose chronological order.

For those gardeners who start their plants from seed, certain essences can be added to the water that is given to the starting trays to help with the germination process.

If you purchase your seedlings from a nursery or commercial greenhouse, it is also a good idea to administer essences to help them get acclimated to their new growing environment.

The next important time to use essences is during the actual transplanting process, when the young plants are taken from their individual pots or trays and put into the ground. In Alaska, this means moving the seedlings out of a nice warm house or greenhouse into the real world of the outside garden where conditions are usually not so moderate.

It is best to make up a transplanting formula that can be used at each stage of the process. Test the plants a few days before they are to be moved to determine which essences will go into the mix. You will want to ask for essences to help the seedlings get over the shock of being transplanted and to help them establish a strong connection with their new environment. This essence formula can be applied before and during the actual transplanting, and at regular intervals for a few days afterwards.

At some point in the life cycle of the garden it may become necessary to use essences to help restore balance between the plant and the insect kingdoms. For many gardeners, this can be a difficult and frustrating time. The overall intent here is to use essences (and other co-creative methods) to establish and maintain a balance of energies within the insect kingdom and within the plant kingdom, as damage to plants from insects is often a response to a weakness or an imbalance in both kingdoms.

If you have a problem in this area it will be necessary to test both the insects and the plants they are eating. If you just treat one side of the situation, then the underlying pattern will not be able to shift into complete balance. Once you have selected the appropriate essences they should be sprayed directly on the plants and insects and added to the watering source. In an extreme situation such as an aphid infestation, essences can be rubbed directly on the affected leaves.

During the summer, essences can be used to facilitate the growth of the garden, especially in those areas where the soil might be depleted or where there are other factors affecting the health of the plants. The basic questions to ask here are: what do the different plants need with regard to the four elements of air (circulation), earth (soil, nutrients), fire (sunlight, heat), and water?

Essences can also be used in emergency situations. Perhaps an animal has broken into the garden and damaged a few plants, or a late frost has hit–both common occurrences in Alaska. In these instances it may be necessary to test each affected plant to see which essences are needed.

Essences and House Plants

Plants that have found their way into our homes often enjoy a greater degree of connection with humans than do plants growing in the garden. This distinction is similar to the one between the group soul level and the individuated level, as mentioned in the preceding section on animal care. Many people have had the same plants in their homes for years. Therefore, the problems that may manifest with these plants can be treated on a more individual basis, rather than on a group level as in the garden.

As stated in the gardening section, essences can be applied to plants to help them receive the elemental nurturing they need to remain healthy. However, when treating house plants we also need to take into consideration the health of the house itself. A house plant that is exhibiting problems is often just reflecting an imbalance present in its surroundings and until that imbalance is addressed, the plant will continue to bring it to our attention.

Another important consideration in this area is the human factor. Plant care is a responsibility that requires a certain level of sensitivity and a willingness to communicate with the plants about their needs. If we want to be able to provide the best care possible, we may need to test ourselves for essences that will help us develop our sensitivity and attunement skills.

Specific information on which essences may be best suited for gardening and plant care can be found under the headings of **Attunement, Awareness, Communication, Gardening**, and **Nature** in Part Seven of this book.

Part Three

The
Alaskan Flower Essences

My highest truth is reflected in all that I see.
I clearly perceive what is here in this moment.

ALDER *Alnus crispa*

Alder grows as a tall, spreading shrub in birch, aspen, and spruce forests, and is also prolific in subalpine areas where its growth habit is nearly impenetrable. In the spring the male catkins elongate to release an abundance of yellow pollen to be born on the wind.

This tree is one of the most important pioneers in the Alaskan landscape. It has root nodules that contain blue-green algae which convert nitrogen from the air into a solid nutrient that enriches the soil. This enables alder to thrive in poor soil where other trees can't grow, and pave the way for others to follow.

Alder ranges from the interior of Alaska eastward across Canada to Greenland.

Indications—unable to see the deeper meaning in life's lessons; taking life at surface value; limited perception of what is true and good for oneself; unable to see what one senses to be true; inability to respond to life's challenges in a way that supports the manifestation of one's highest potential.

Healing Qualities—Throughout our lives, we are continually presented with opportunities that are designed to facilitate the learning of those lessons that we agreed to take on in this lifetime. Our challenge is to clearly and correctly sense the form and content of each learning opportunity as it is given, so that we can respond in a way that is in alignment with our highest truth.

However, our ability to see and to translate the essence of what we see into appropriate action is often influenced by our past experiences and by our current belief systems. These influences act as filters that limit what we are capable of seeing, consequently limiting our ability to respond to each life situation or lesson in a way that truly supports our learning process.

It is in this context that the Alder essence can be applied. Alder brings a new level of lucidity to our seeing by helping us access light and information that exists beyond our normal range of perception. This essence helps us experience a clarity of physical sight that is simultaneously enriched with an increased level of knowing. It is this ability to see and know the truth of a situation in the moment that empowers us to move beyond our limiting mental programming and respond to any learning opportunity in a way that supports our soul's evolution.

I unconditionally accept the totality of who I AM.
My heart is open to the generous, loving energy of the planet.

ALPINE AZALEA *Loiseleuria procumbens*

Alpine Azalea is a trailing evergreen shrub which generally grows in mats up to a yard square and one to two inches tall. The leaves are 1/8 to 1/4 inches long by 1/16 inches wide, and grow from multi-branched twigs.

The tiny flowers occur in clusters at the end of the twigs on short stalks. The corolla is bell shaped and pink in color, although white sometimes occurs.

Alpine Azalea flowers from late May through early July, its fruits maturing in July and August. It is common on well-drained rocky sites in arctic and alpine tundra and is widespread in the mountains and high tundra throughout Alaska.

Indications—self-doubt; low self-esteem; unable to love or accept certain parts of oneself; withholding love from oneself and therefore from others; lacking compassion for oneself and others.

Healing Qualities—This essence is for those who live in a attitude of conditional self-acceptance. This attitude maintains an imbalance deep within the heart which prevents our vital life force energies from entering and circulating throughout all parts of the physical body.

The Alpine Azalea essence connects us with the vibration of love as it is present in all the kingdoms of nature. As we open our hearts to this penetrating vibration, it is able to catalyze the release of old patterns of self-doubt. As each pattern is released, corresponding parts of the body are able to come into balance, and the overall flow of vital life energy within us is strengthened.

This essence helps us create an unconditional level of self-understanding and compassion in our lives. As we learn to hold the totality of who we are in a loving regard, we are able to draw more and more of the spirit of love into our bodies, where it can serve as a powerful source of healing for ourselves and others.

My life energy flows freely and abundantly throughout
my physical body.
My body rhythms are in harmony with the
natural cycles of the planet.

BALSAM POPLAR *Populus balsamifera*

Balsam Poplar is a tall, straight, rapidly growing tree with smooth, grey-green bark that becomes dark, rough, and thickened with age.

The trees are unisexual, which means the male and female flowers occur on different trees. The female trees are extremely prolific, releasing great quantities of cottony seed capsules in June. Not content to rely solely on their abundant seeds for reproduction, balsam poplars produce such high levels of rooting hormones that cut twigs planted in wet ground can take root and grow into trees.

The winter leaf buds are large, pointed, resinous, and give off a pungent odor that permeates the air in spring. Known also as cottonwood, this tree is abundant on river gravels and other well drained habitats such as south facing hillsides.

Indications—sexual and emotional tension and dysfunction; infertility; difficulties with menstruation; menstrual cycles of uneven duration which are not synchronized with moon cycles; inconsistent emotional and sexual response; shock and trauma from sexual abuse.

Healing Qualities—The physical characteristics of this tree display important clues to its healing qualities. The heady fragrance of sticky buds opening on a warm spring day, the deep red pendulous catkins, and the rapid growth rate of the tree all give expression to an abundant and naturally occurring quality of fertile life force energy.

The Balsam Poplar essence is a catalyst for the release of deeply held emotional and sexual tensions. These blockages limit the circulation of sexual and creative energies in our physical bodies, and their healthy expression in our lives. Balsam Poplar stimulates a flow of healing energy to those areas of the body that are holding these tensions, and helps us understand the issues responsible for them. As these blockages are released, we are better able to re-synchronize our internal body rhythms with natural lunar and planetary cycles.

Balsam Poplar is particularly helpful for those who have experienced some sort of sexual or physical abuse during their lives, especially when the trauma from such an experience has begun to affect the functioning of the body in some way. In such instances, the essence can also be used externally, by adding it to massage oil or to the bath, to help release this trauma from the body.

The truth of who I am is eternally present in my consciousness.
The eternal wisdom of the ages is alive within every
cell of my body.

BLACK SPRUCE *Picea mariana*

Black Spruce is an evergreen tree inhabiting bogs, lake margins, muskegs, and north-facing slopes throughout the interior of Alaska.

Although they can grow up to 30 feet tall on the warmer, south-facing hillsides, black spruce are characteristically short trees where their roots encounter permafrost, or permanently frozen ground. They are the natural bonsai of the boreal forest, where a 100 year old tree may be only 20 feet tall.

The branches of this tree are short, sparse, and slightly drooping at the ends. This spruce is easily identified by the black or brown hairs on the twigs between the needles. The female cones are small and egg-shaped, and remain in clusters at the tree tops for years. This essence was prepared using male and female cones, which occur together on the same trees.

Indications—contracted view of life; oblivious to the wisdom and awareness of others; tendency to forget the lessons and information learned from past experiences; difficulty applying one's knowledge and wisdom to one's present circumstances.

Healing Qualities—Black Spruce is a powerful symbol of the unitive consciousness that exists within the plant kingdom. This quality is illustrated by its unique family signature. Clusters of black spruce are common because the lower branches often take root to form a ring of small trees around the parent tree. This method of vegetative reproduction helps the trees propagate between the occurrences of fire, the only event that opens and releases seeds from the cones. This rooting system also serves to energetically link all of the trees in each family together in consciousness.

Black Spruce represents the ancient grandfather energy of nature. Its essence helps us open our perceptions to the wisdom that is present within each of us and within the collective consciousness of the planet. It helps us connect more fully with the eternal aspects of who we are, and in particular, with information learned from past lessons that we need to remember or reactivate in the context of our present life situations.

This essence is also an important aid to meditation and attunement. It can be used to help families or other groups of people meditate and attune together, and will be particularly beneficial when the intention of this exercise is to receive information that will be valuable to each individual and the group as a whole.

My inner knowing shatters all illusion; my inner sight is clear.
I bask in the pure light of Truth.

BLADDERWORT *Utricularia vulgaris*

Bladderwort is an aquatic carnivorous plant with unique eating habits. Its bright flowers are supported by a single upright stem, which is in turn supported by modified leaves and roots which form a radial pattern under the water.

Along the stems of these modified underwater roots are bladders which constitute the carnivorous portion of the plant. They operate through the use of trigger hairs which are activated by the various waterborne life forms as they swim by. When stimulated, these hairs cause the bladders to open up and draw in the insects. In this way the plant supplements its diet, which it needs to do because it grows in a nutrient poor environment.

Indications—unable to see the truth at the core of an issue; easily deceived or taken advantage of; lacking discernment when faced with dishonesty in others; unable to make decisions that support one's highest good.

Healing Qualities—Bladderwort is for those who are actively seeking clarity and truth, as it supports the development of a level of inner knowing that can be drawn upon to illuminate all areas of our lives.

The essence of this unique flower strengthens and supports our ability to perceive that which lies at the core of an issue or situation, regardless of the illusory energies that might be surrounding it. Illusion is a network of energy made up of all the thoughts and feelings that surround a given circumstance. The saying that you can't see the forest for the trees is very applicable here. We often can't see the truth because of all the preconceived notions we have of what it should look like.

Bladderwort also addresses the issue of discernment. It is a common occurrence in our world to be faced with dishonesty in others, and to allow ourselves to be blinded or deceived by the illusions that others project in our direction. If we lack clear insight and keen judgement in such situations, it will be difficult to distinguish which actions will serve our highest good.

Regardless of the source of our bewilderment, the essence of Bladderwort can work with our perceptions to create a higher perspective that will enable us to penetrate through any energy that is confusing an issue, to the truth that lies at its center. The healing message of Bladderwort is clear: the truth is simple–it is only the web of illusion around it that is complex. Dissolve this web and we are left with the simple beauty of the truth.

I easily expand on all levels of my being to accommodate
the abundance of the universe.
I deserve to receive all that I need to live my life
to its full potential.

BLUEBERRY POLLEN *Vaccinium uliginosum*

This essence was prepared as a sun infusion using only the pollen bearing anthers of the bog blueberry flowers. Pollen essences differ from flower essences in that they contain the highest magnetic frequencies of energy that a given plant is capable of transmitting. They can be used to help us move deeper into those issues and life lessons that we have already started to heal with flower essences.

Indications—low prosperity consciousness; issues of unworthiness and low self-esteem; lack of belief in the concept of abundance; expecting the worst to happen; difficulty receiving from others; having a contracted rather than an expansive experience of life.

Healing Qualities—Alaska is an immense land of great power and purity. There are a relatively small number of plant species present here, but several dominant species enjoy an extensive range covering millions of acres. Blueberries comprise one of the largest and most prolific plant communities that reside in this vast environment.

This abundant presence of the blueberry plant catalyzes an ongoing renewal of cosmic and earth energies in the environment, supporting on a grand scale the well-being of all life in this subarctic region of the Earth. The Blueberry Pollen essence works in much the same way for humans, by encouraging us to expand on all levels to accommodate the abundance of universal energy available to us in every moment of our lives.

This essence helps us identify and release deeply held beliefs that support the idea that we do not deserve to have all that we require to live our lives to their full potential. These limiting thoughts have powerful energy fields that interfere with our ability to receive. Therefore, as long as we remain attached to them, we will be unable to manifest all the energy and abundance we deserve.

It is the high magnetic energy of the pollen in this essence that helps us penetrate, break down, and release these interference patterns so we can attract and receive all that we require to live our lives to their fullest.

I understand the seeds of my anger and release them into love.
What I feel, I can heal.

BLUE ELF VIOLA *Viola sp.*

Blue Elf Violas are a hardy addition to any Alaskan garden. They begin to flower in late May and resist the early fall freezes, continuing to give color to the garden into September and early October.

These plants grow over a foot tall and bloom abundantly. The small flowers are deep purple with dark stripes leading into a bright orange-yellow center.

Indications—emotional repression; unable to get in touch with and process deep-seated anger, rage, and frustration; unable to express anger in a clear, nonviolent way; difficulty resolving conflicts, especially in group situations.

Healing Qualities—The calming vibrations of these cheerful flowers support the process of understanding and releasing deeply held anger and frustration.

Anger is a healthy, cleansing part of our life force which needs to flow freely. When it is suppressed or bottled up, a lot of our own vital energy is used to keep it in place. The Blue Elf Viola essence helps us dissipate the layers of protective energy we have built up around our anger and frustrations, so that we may gain a better understanding of the core feelings at the root of these emotions and allow them to be released.

The essence of Blue Elf Viola brings the energy and understanding of the heart into this process, enabling us to express our anger in a clear but nonviolent way, forgive those responsible (including ourselves), and bring the whole emotional cycle to completion.

This essence is also valuable in resolving group conflict, helping those involved diffuse the emotional energy charge that is connected to the issues being discussed. This energy can then be released back to the group in a positive way and support a more graceful resolution of the situation.

I unconditionally welcome the abundance of the Universe
into my life.
The bounty of the Universe flows through me
without limitation.

BOG BLUEBERRY *Vaccinium uliginosum*

Bog Blueberry is a many branched shrub growing from one to two feet high. The leaves are oval shaped and a bright green in color.

Numerous flowers grow from the ends or sides of slender, round twigs on nodding stalks. The corolla is urn shaped and dark pink in color. This variety of blueberry flowers in June. Its dark blue berries ripen in late July and early August, and are picked in large quantities by bears, birds, and people.

Bog Blueberry is a very common and widespread shrub occurring in bogs, open forest, and tundra habitats throughout Alaska.

Indications—stagnation; resistance to life; conditional acceptance of abundance; attachment to the way or form in which prosperity manifests in one's life; holding back one's creative energies.

Healing Qualities—The essence of Bog Blueberry works with the issue of blocking the experience of abundance. Prosperity comes when one doesn't resist the flow of life. This essence helps us dissolve thought patterns and belief systems that hold our interactions with life in stagnation.

Bog Blueberry helps us identify those areas in our minds where we let our attachment to form limit our experience of abundance–where we block the abundance that is available to us by not accepting the form in which it has chosen to appear.

This inflexibility not only stops the fullness of life from reaching us, it also prevents our creative energies from reaching others, and when this energy is not circulated everyone loses out.

This essence helps us open our minds so that the bounty of the universe can flow through us without limitation. It teaches us to unconditionally accept the abundance that is offered, and give the appropriate response for what we receive through a conscious attitude of gratitude.

As I trust, I am healed.
I live in a safe universe.

BOG ROSEMARY *Andromeda polifolia*

Bog Rosemary is an attractive evergreen dwarf shrub with a creeping base and occasionally branched stems. Leaves are alternate, thick and leathery, grayish green above and whitish below. The globe shaped flowers hang singly from the end of each branch. The corolla is generally up to 3/8 inch long and urn shaped.

Bog Rosemary is almost completely circumpolar in range, and is widespread in Alaska except on the Aleutian Islands, occurring in peat bogs and swamps. It flowers from early June in the northern locations, to mid-July in southern habitats.

Indications—immobilized by fears of the unknown; inability to take risks in order to grow or heal; always questioning why things are the way they are; difficulty accepting support or assistance from others because of a lack of trust in them.

Healing Qualities—Any true experience of transformation requires us to transcend our known reality and venture into previously unexplored parts of ourselves. Our ability to move into and occupy this new inner space can often be blocked by our fears of the unknown which are held deep within our hearts.

The essence of Bog Rosemary strengthens the virtue of trust. It extends its energy to our hearts in a way that enables us to feel divine support while being present with our deepest fears. When we bring the light of awareness to a place where fear is held, it is released. Each time we are able to confront and embrace a new part of ourselves in this way, we allow a deeper penetration of the light. This action builds more trust–in ourselves, and in the light.

The Bog Rosemary essence also addresses the habit many of us have of getting caught up in the outer manifestations of our healing processes. We live on the physical plane. Therefore, most, if not all, of our life lessons will involve other people and situations outside of ourselves. We become distracted by these outside involvements when we forget that they were created to bring attention to a part of our inner self that is calling out to be healed.

Bog Rosemary asks us to not question or get caught up in the outer form of the lessons life provides, but rather to place unlimited trust in the inner processes with which we are involved. In this way, we allow divine healing support to move into all areas of our lives, and through all the people and situations we encounter.

My mind is one with heart and will.
I unconditionally accept the Divine order of life.

BUNCHBERRY *Cornus canadensis*

Bunchberry is an attractive member of the dogwood family. It is often propagated as an ornamental ground cover for its showy flowers and bronze/purple fall coloring.

This plant has erect stems four to eight inches high, and usually four to six bright green leaves that form a whorl beneath the inflorescence. The tiny "true" flowers form tight clusters in the center of a flower head. They are surrounded by four or more cream colored petal-like bracts, or modified leaves. The fruits are clusters of bright red berries.

Bunchberry is a common ground cover in the moist spruce forests of Alaska. It is also widespread throughout Canada, and east to Greenland.

Indications—lack of mental focus, easily distracted by the activities of others; unable to concentrate on the work at hand; difficulty completing demanding tasks and projects; easily caught up in the emotional turmoil of others.

Healing Qualities—This essence is for individuals who are easily distracted, who lack the concentration required to complete a mentally demanding task, and for those who are unable to maintain their internal focus during times of emotional conflict or turmoil.

The essence of Bunchberry encourages mental strength and clarity. Its vibration acts as a catalyst that helps us bring our mental energies into alignment with divine will so that we may experience higher levels of concentration and focus.

This essence encourages us to unconditionally accept the inherent order of life. As we learn to practice this quality of acceptance, we begin to waste less time and energy being distracted by those things that appear to be outside our sphere of mental control. We begin to see that what is really distracting us is our mind, which seizes on one aspect of something to the exclusion of another. Once we release this pattern of distraction, our mental energies are free to operate at higher levels of clarity and efficiency.

The Bunchberry essence also helps us strengthen the boundary between our mental and emotional bodies. When this boundary is intact, we are better able to maintain our concentration and focus on matters at hand, despite the emotional turmoil that we or those around us might be feeling.

I perceive the joy of nature within my own life essence.
Surrounded by stillness, I notice the finer details of life.

CASSANDRA *Chamaedaphne calyculata*

Cassandra is a low evergreen shrub, usually growing two to three feet tall. It has dark green leaves which are thick, leathery and slightly rolled under at the edges. The flowers occur in a row on short stalks and hang down on the lower side of the stems; the corolla is white and cylindrical.

Cassandra is one of the first plants to bloom in the interior of Alaska. It flowers in early to late May, usually before the leaves of other plants have emerged. In the fall, winter, and spring, the leaves of this plant have a reddish color, giving many bogs this hue when viewed from a distance.

Cassandra is abundant in wetlands and open black spruce stands throughout most of Alaska.

Indications—difficulty shifting one's attention and perspective from the outer world to one's inner world; unable to relax into a meditative state or reach deeper levels of meditation; lack of awareness of the subtleties of nature.

Healing Qualities—Cassandra is an essence that can dramatically improve the quality of our relationship with nature. This essence encourages stillness of mind. It can be used as an aid to meditation, to help us receive inner guidance, and especially as a catalyst to help us connect more fully with the environment in our attunements with nature.

Cassandra promotes a kind of sensory relaxation that allows our perceptual focus to turn inward and become aligned with the ebb and flow of our own life essence. From this perspective we are able to approach the boundaries of our perceptions, and then move beyond them into more profound levels of recognition.

This shift in the focus and depth of our perceptions enables us to sense the currents of life on a much deeper and more encompassing level, and enter into a more graceful and co-creative relationship with our environment.

The truth of my destiny resonates clearly
within my being.
The power of my Divine essence is eternally present.

CATTAIL POLLEN *Typha latifolia*

Cattails are an easily identifiable plant for most. Their swordlike leaves and tall flower spikes can grow up to nine feet high. The upper male flowers produce an abundance of yellow pollen and then fall off. The lower female flower spikes change from a bright green to brown at maturity and split open to yield an abundance of down-like seeds.

Cattails flourish near shallow lakes, marshes, and on the edges of ponds. This essence was prepared as a sun infusion using only the pollen from the male flowers.

Indications—letting oneself be talked into doing things that are not in one's highest good; difficulty standing up for oneself, especially when one encounters obstacles or challenges to one's chosen life path; weakened by old patterns of pain or trauma, and by old energy connections that no longer serve one's highest truth.

Healing Qualities—There are times when great strength is required to live our lives in accordance with our highest purpose, especially when we encounter deeply held patterns of trauma, resistance, pain, and fear. We often let the existence of such energies stop and invalidate the real progress we have been making in our lives. When this happens we need to call on the validation that comes from a strong and conscious connection with our divine essence.

The power of our divine essence is always there, but it is often difficult to keep our hearts and perceptions open to its existence so that we can draw upon it in times of need. Cattail Pollen embodies a highly magnetic quality of energy that aligns and energizes all of our chakras and penetrates through our pain and trauma to reveal our eternal self. Empowered with this new vision and vitality, we can once again set out on our chosen path, standing tall in our truth, with a clear view of the potential that lies ahead.

Furthermore, as our consciousness grows and our life perspective changes, it is logical that our support systems–our circles of friends and counselors, will need to change as well. This is often a confusing and difficult process. Cattail Pollen can make it easier by helping us to strongly project our true selves out into the world so we can attract people that resonate with us at that level. The stability that we can derive from this will be invaluable as we go through these times of transition, as it will be much easier to move through our own changes if we are supported by the harmonious energies of others.

I joyously celebrate my physical existence.
I open my heart to the loving energy of the Divine Mother.

CHIMING BELLS *Mertensia paniculata*

Chiming Bells is a perennial herb occurring in wet areas in meadows and woods, shady roadsides and stream banks. It often grows in extensive clumps of curving stems up to three feet tall.

The flowers occur in clusters at the ends of the stems, their color a deep purplish blue, the young unopened ones having a pink cast. These attractive flowers are found throughout Alaska except the North Slope and Aleutian Islands.

Indications—sad; discouraged; despondent; worn out; no joy in one's day-to-day existence; feeling out of touch with life and with one's inner sense of direction; feeling a lack of support and stability at a basic level; heart feels unprotected.

Healing Qualities—Chiming Bells is a plant of significance in the area of Earth healing, specifically in the cycle of renewal that takes place after a forest fire. It will often move into and become the dominant plant in recently burned areas, where it will assist in the rebuilding of the soil on an energy level. It will then allow other plants to establish themselves to continue the cycle of regrowth and regeneration.

Chiming Bells is an important essence for regeneration and renewal in humans as well. It is an essence for those who feel out of touch with their own inner dynamics and for those who have lost track of who they are in the course of all the changes and transformations of their lives.

Chiming Bells brings a tonic and uplifting energy to the heart, helping us reconnect with our own true thoughts, feelings, and life direction. It helps us reestablish peace and stability at the physical level of our beings, and open our lives once again to the experience of joy in physical existence, an experience that is our birthright.

But most importantly, the essence of Chiming Bells is a vibrational bridge that helps us connect with a real and tangible source of support that is available to us at all times, no matter how lost we feel–the loving energy of the Divine Mother. As we allow this energy to penetrate and strengthen our hearts, we gain hope, courage, and a new found sense of trust in our ability to move forward in joy and love.

I am a miracle of creation.
I live in full appreciation of my unique beauty.

COLUMBINE *Aquilegia formosa*

This columbine is commonly referred to as Western or Red Columbine. Its showy flowers range from moist woods to mountain meadows and slopes throughout the southern half of Alaska, British Columbia, and northwestern United States. Wild and cultivated columbines are also favorites with gardeners.

Indications—self-effacing; weak sense of self; unable to see one's own unique or distinctive beauty; judging one's appearance by superficial standards; hiding one's inner beauty and sweetness from others.

Healing Qualities—Painted in colors of red and gold, and blessed with nectar as sweet as a kiss, columbine is distinctive, and often considered "beautiful". Yet its form, color, and proportions are uniquely different from those of most other flowers.

Physical beauty is often measured by comparative standards, such as a person's weight or hair color. Columbine is beautiful in that it's perfectly itself, expressing itself in a natural fashion.

People often dislike their reflection because they see themselves as failing to meet artificial measures of beauty. Columbine is a reminder to be as nature guides you to be, to be uniquely yourself and to appreciate that uniqueness, regardless of how it differs from the norm. Just as columbine contains nectar hidden in its swollen tips, so too will you discover the sweetness of yourself within.

The essence of Columbine is for strengthening our sense of self, of who we really are, and for allowing that truth to radiate into our world without concern. This flower asks us to not hide our beauty from others, but rather to send a powerful projection of who we are out into the world for all to see.

My perceptions are grounded in wisdom and love.
I open my heart to the future.

COMANDRA *Geocaulon lividum*

Comandra flowers are small and pale green, each with approximately four petals. They occur in little geometric clusters of three and five to a plant and often bloom early, before the leaves have fully emerged on their stems.

Comandra occurs in birch and aspen forests throughout the interior of Alaska.

Indications—out of touch with one's environment; unaware of the subtler energies that exist in nature; focus of one's perceptions limited to the gross, material aspects of the physical world; difficulty translating awareness of higher dimensional energies into third dimensional understanding.

Healing Qualities—This essence is a valuable tool for those who are just embarking on a process of developing their inner awareness of the subtle worlds of nature. It is also helpful for those who would like to deepen their attunement with specific plant energies for the purpose of healing.

At this time in the history and evolution of our planet, it is of prime importance that the human race consciously join in a co-creative partnership with nature. Nature is ready for this partnership, but the human kingdom faces a challenge of perception–the task of learning to really see and hear nature. In order to meet this challenge we must be willing to relinquish our all-consuming focus on the gross aspects of the physical world, and begin to extend our perceptions and deepen our awareness to include the finer and subtler energies that exist in our natural surroundings. The Comandra essence is a facilitator in this process. It operates within our energy system to clear perceptual blockages that interfere with our ability to sense and experience the various levels of subtle energy that exist within the plant kingdom.

Comandra is also helpful for those who are very sensitive to higher dimensions of reality but are having difficulty translating what they perceive on those levels into practical and useful information in the here and now.

The capacity to see that which exists beyond the physical world is a function of the 6th chakra. Difficulties arise when the visionary activities of this chakra are not grounded into the physical body. Comandra addresses this difficulty by linking the perceptive ability of the 6th chakra with the wisdom of the heart. When these two centers are connected energetically as well as in consciousness, our full visionary potential can be realized.

I exchange my pain for awareness and understanding.
I focus on what is being healed in this moment.

COTTON GRASS *Eriophorum sp.*

Cotton Grass forms stands of solitary stems up to 12 inches high that rise from a thin, creeping rootstock. It is well known by the modified sepals and petals of tiny flowers, which form a wooly tuft at the top of the stem that resembles cotton.

Cotton Grass, or Alaska Cotton as it is sometimes called, is common in marshy, peaty locations, often growing in shallow water around the edge of ponds. It can be found throughout Alaska and is circumpolar in range.

Indications—shock and trauma resulting from an accident or injury; unable to shift one's perspective from pain or injury to the progression of one's healing process; unable to completely heal an old injury because of a lack of awareness of the deeper issues that led to its creation.

Healing Qualities —Cotton Grass plays an integral part in naturally occurring events of transformation and renewal. A potent example from nature is wildfire. Forest fires respond to a need in the environment for dynamic change by literally burning out the old patterns of energy that are present. This dramatic shift encourages Cotton Grass, along with other plants such as fireweed and chiming bells, to take root in the burned area and begin the process of regrowth and regeneration.

The essence of Cotton Grass works in a similar way with humans. It is often indicated for those who have suffered a traumatic accident in their past and are still holding on to the shock and trauma from that experience.

Cotton Grass helps seal energy breaks in the aura which often accompany injuries, and can be applied topically where there has been a trauma to the physical body. But more importantly, this essence helps a person move their focus from the pain and shock they experienced in the past, to the process of healing that is taking place in the present moment.

This essence helps one come to a deeper understanding of the issues that still need to be resolved, issues that in some way led to the creation of their accident or injury in the first place. Once a person has this understanding, they are better able to release whatever pain and trauma they are still holding and bring the whole learning and healing process to completion.

I fully accept the perfection of this moment.
I move gracefully with the winds of change.

COW PARSNIP *Heracleum lanatum*

Cow Parsnip is a perennial plant of fields and roadsides that often reaches 9 feet in height. It is a member of the Umbelliferae (parsley) family and is characterized by umbrella-shaped flowers, stout, hollow stems, and dinner plate-sized palmate leaves. "Pushki" is the common Russian name for this herb.

Indications—difficulty connecting with or adapting to new surroundings after a move; not sure of one's inner direction; feeling cut off from one's roots; unable to settle down anywhere; feeling caught up in the confusion and chaos of the times.

Healing Qualities—Cow Parsnip's genus name, Heracleum, honors Hercules; its specific name lanatum means "wooly".

This essence is ideal for those who are drifting from place to place, who have no place to call home, and who feel powerless to direct their lives. It heightens awareness of inner strength, promotes a sense of contentment with the present moment, and encourages peace of mind, even during times of transition and change.

Hercules traveled widely during his twelve labors. Cow Parsnip is also a wide traveler, ranging from central Alaska to the southwestern United States and eastward to Newfoundland. It offers us an appropriate essence for these times, especially for travelers and for those relocating from one part of the country to another, as it assists with the process of adapting to a new environment.

Like the mythological god Hercules, this plant is stately and strong. Its wide range, stout physical structure and robust growth rate are evidence of Cow Parsnip's ability to put down roots and thrive in a variety of different locations and habitats. Its message is: it is not where we are, but the strength and depth of our connection that is important.

Cow Parsnip helps us create a sense of being at home anywhere on the planet by helping us master the qualities of flexibility and adaptation. It is through an awareness and acceptance of the perfection of each present moment that we are able to access the support and energy we need, wherever we are, and translate this into strength and stability in our daily lives.

I replace tension with awareness and communication.
I meet turmoil and stress with gentle strength and endurance.

DANDELION *Taraxacum officinale*

Dandelion is a well known perennial herb featuring bright yellow flowers which grow in single heads on slender, hollow stems three to ten inches high. Its name is French, meaning, "the tooth of the lion", and is descriptive of the toothed margins of the leaves. The number of incisions in the leaves are indicative of the amount of sunlight the plant gets.

Dandelion is very abundant because of its special methods of insuring survival. These include deeply growing roots, bitter tasting leaves, and seed "umbrellas" which travel easily on the wind.

Known since ancient times, dandelion continues to play an important role in modern folk medicine. The species name officinale means that the plant has been recognized as an official healing agent. Dandelion is found in moist, waste places, along roadsides, and in yards throughout Alaska.

Indications—hardness; obstinacy; chronic muscle tension; unaware of the deeper mental attitudes and emotional issues that are creating tension in one's body; having difficulty getting in touch with and releasing emotional energy stored in the body.

Healing Qualities—During times of turmoil and stress, the Dandelion essence can help us remain connected to our inner qualities of gentle strength and endurance. We are reminded by the signature of the plant that these attributes become more deeply rooted through exposure to adverse circumstances–Dandelion has survived in bright abundance despite continual attempts at eradication by those who consider it a weed.

Dandelion helps us endure stress and conflict with an attitude of softness and flexibility rather than hardness and obstinacy, qualities that can lead to a buildup of tension in the physical body.

When taken internally, this essence can help us improve the quality of communication we have with our body, so that we are better able to identify and understand the issues that lie at the core of our patterns of tension. At the same time, the Dandelion essence can be applied externally to those areas of the body that chronically hold these patterns. This dual method of application is an efficient way to release the muscle tension that is present in the body, and the underlying mental and emotional issues that contribute to its formation.

I open my innermost being to cleansing, transformation,
and renewal.
I bless the old and embrace the new.

FIREWEED *Epilobium angustifolium*

Fireweed has a tremendous visual impact in Alaska with its tall stems, brightly colored flowers, and one of the longest blossoming periods of any plant in the state. This hardy plant displays a unique pattern of growth: the magenta blossoms open successively, going up the stem, the lower flowers opening first. This flowering pattern gives us a visual symbol of Fireweed's healing qualities as it displays the continual movement of energy through successive stages of growth.

Fireweed has a very efficient reproductive system with creeping rootstalks and easily dispersed seeds. These are covered in a fluffy hair which enables them to be carried great distances by the wind. This species of Fireweed ranges over extensive areas of the state on the disturbed soils of roadsides, and in meadows, forests, and recently burned areas.

Indications—ungrounded; energy stagnation on any level; needing to release pain, shock, and trauma resulting from an accident or injury; feeling burned-out; weak vertical connection between the Earth and the spiritual realms; attempting to carry the past into the future.

Healing Qualities—Fireweed is a unique plant in terms of Earth healing due to its tremendous range and ability to come into disturbed environments, especially burned over areas, and form an etheric network of restorative energy. The vibration of this plant merges with the vibration of the soil, cleansing and renewing its pattern and enabling it to attract new plant life.

The Fireweed essence does much the same for our human forms, stimulating the renewal of energies on all levels of our beings. It is a powerful catalyst for growth and transformation that encourages us to release anything that is no longer appropriate or useful in our lives, so that we can create new experiences free from the limitations of the past.

This essence is particularly important for those who have burned up their vital life energies through prolonged struggle or misuse. Fireweed helps such persons let go of the habits and patterns of behavior that contributed to their state of exhaustion, and replace them with a new matrix of connection to the Earth and the etheric realms.

Fireweed is also very useful in emergency situations. It facilitates the release of pain, trauma, and discomfort from our bodies, supports our self healing abilities, and helps us attract restorative healing energy from our surroundings.

I live in full remembrance of my Divine innocence.
It is now safe for me to release all of my fear.

FORGET-ME-NOT *Myosotis alpestris*

This species of Forget-Me-Not is a bright and enduring addition to the garden, flowering throughout the growing season.

The stems and leaves are covered with short hairs, with those on the stems being dense enough to give them a fuzzy, white appearance. The leaves alternate as they ascend the stem while gradually becoming smaller. The inflorescence extends upward as more flowers develop. Petals are blue or frequently pinkish in color, surrounding a white and yellow center.

Indications—feeling separate from and having difficulty connecting to the spiritual dimension, and to one's spiritual origins; parts of the self seem to be lost or forgotten; deeper connections with others are blocked by subconscious fears; unresolved guilt about past actions; lack of respect for oneself and others.

Healing Qualities—The essence of Forget-Me-Not addresses an all too common malaise in our modern society–the sensation of being disconnected from one's spiritual and creative Source. This separation from something larger than oneself, and from the origins of one's creative impulses, can lead to actions which are disrespectful of the true self, others, and the planet.

This sense of separation is created over time by an accumulation in the subconscious mind of fears, guilt, and the pain from past experiences. The Forget-Me-Not essence helps us create a vibrational pathway to the subconscious mind that allows these energies to flow to the heart, where they can be released creatively and compassionately. The corresponding experiences, and the lessons contained within them, can then be integrated.

Forget-Me-Not helps us remember the moment in time when a dream, a path of action, or a pattern of behavior originated. By contacting the source points of these acts of creation, we are able to bring to our conscious mind an awareness of the pure spiritual impulses that led to their conception. This awareness strengthens our understanding of who we really are by restoring our sense of innocence, and enables us to create our lives with a deeper respect for ourselves, for others, and for the planet Earth.

As I let go of my attachment to the problem, I see the solution.
I bless this moment with total acceptance.

FOXGLOVE *Digitalis purpurea*

Foxglove flowers are born on a three to five foot stalk that rises from a basal arrangement of large, broadly-lanced shaped leaves. They bloom from the base upwards with perhaps ten or more flowers opening at a time. The lightly fragrant flowers occur in shades of carmine, pink, cream, white, and maroon, and are distinctively spotted on the lower half leading into the corolla.

Indications—mental inflexibility; attached to seeing things a certain way; emotional and physical tension and constriction, especially around the heart; lacking perspective on how to deal with a situation or conflict; unable to see the lesson or issue at the heart of a problem.

Healing Qualities—This essence is for when we find ourselves in a situation where we have lost all perspective and have no idea of how to proceed. It is particularly useful when we experience fear that is so strong that our perceptions close down and we don't know what to do or which way to go, and the more we identify with our unpleasant predicament, the stronger these feelings get.

Foxglove relieves the energetic tension around the heart that accompanies this kind of experience. As this tension is released, our breathing opens up and our energy flow is restored. At the same time, Foxglove expands our perspective so that we can see through our fear and transform the underlying thoughts, feelings, and belief systems that are responsible for it.

This essence empowers us to live our lives without the fear of taking emotional risks in our relationships. It helps us strengthen our hearts so they can open, instead of contracting or closing down, in response to a conflict or challenge. But the strongest message from Foxglove is that while fear is real, love is bigger–and the quickest way to move through any kind of fear is to open our hearts to love. As we put this truth into action in our lives, we gain the confidence that we can meet whatever comes our way with penetrating insight and compassionate understanding.

My unified creative energies attract exactly what I need
in each moment.
I integrate each new experience with focus and ease.

GOLDEN CORYDALIS *Corydalis aurea*

Golden Corydalis is a sprawling, multi-branched plant displaying an abundance of bright, golden flowers. These flowers have a unique, pouched shaped upper petal and become visible in June, their fruits maturing in July and August.

Golden Corydalis is found in moist places in open woods, thickets, gravelly roadsides, and lake margins, mainly in the interior portions of Alaska.

Indications—scattered or chaotic personality; overwhelmed by and unable to integrate new experiences; cannot make sense of how one's experiences fit together; cannot get all of one's talents and skills to work together in a focused way.

Healing Qualities—Golden Corydalis helps a person establish and maintain a spiritual point of reference, a link with the higher self that will help them attract, organize, and integrate their life experience according to the needs of the soul.

This essence speaks directly to those people who have lost the ability to easily integrate and assimilate life experiences because of a breakdown in communications between the personality and the higher self.

This breakdown often results when an individual becomes overwhelmed by the pace and intensity of life, and begins to compartmentalize those aspects of experience that cannot be easily understood. This practice interrupts the communication that would normally take place between an experience and the consciousness that created it. As a result, the person no longer feels overwhelmed by that experience. However, as this practice continues, each new experience becomes increasingly difficult to integrate.

Golden Corydalis works to reverse this process. It helps the individual restore full communications between the soul and personality levels of consciousness and all of those experiences that have yet to be integrated. Once this link has been reestablished, they are better able to connect with, understand, and absorb the information at the heart of each experience, and integrate that experience into the whole.

I am connected to the Source of all Light.
In this moment I lovingly accept the nourishment of Light
into every cell of my body.

GRASS OF PARNASSUS *Parnassia palustris*

These delicate and fragrant flowers grow atop slim, smooth stems. Each stem has a single bract about halfway up and long, heart-shaped basal leaves. The blossoms consist of five white petals which are marked with greenish veins. The genus name of this flower is derived from the Grecian Mount Parnassus. This species is circumpolar, except for Greenland, and occurs throughout most of the state in wet meadows, tundra, and along lake shores.

Indications—difficulty maintaining the integrity of one's energy field in crowded or polluted environments; needing to cleanse and recharge one's aura, especially after a deeply transformational healing experience; meditation or healing space needs to be cleansed and reenergized.

Healing Qualities—This flower offers a fountain of white light that is nourishing to all levels of our being. Its energy is effervescent, joyful, uplifting and liberating.

Grass of Parnassus is an essence to use whenever we feel the need to cleanse and charge our energy fields. It brings a very high and pure quality of light into the aura, and can be used to help one attune more clearly to higher frequencies of energy. It is an effective essence to use when preparing oneself for meditation, and can also be used to cleanse the meditation room.

Grass of Parnassus is also an excellent essence for massage practitioners to use during and after a session. It promotes a greater energy flow in both client and therapist, and helps to neutralize and recharge the energy of the therapy room.

This powerful essence is especially helpful for those who choose to live and do their work in crowded or polluted surroundings, as it brings an increased level of protection to the human energy system while helping it attract increased levels of energetic nourishment from nature.

Grass of Parnassus also has a distinct family signature. It can assist groups of individuals who are working together for a higher purpose, where it is important that each person's light be allowed to shine brightly within the larger dynamic.

I am at home on this Earth.
My heart and mind are open to the beauty and intelligence that
exists in nature.

GREEN BELLS OF IRELAND *Molucella laevis*

Green Bells of Ireland is a strikingly unusual member of the mint family. It is highly fragrant with a pungent scent that distinguishes it from all other garden plants.

The green bell-like calyces develop by midsummer with the actual flowers appearing in early fall. Before the flowers open only a small, fuzzy, pink cap is visible at the center of the green bell. This cap unfolds to become the upper flower petal while the lower petal opens out to expose a cleft lip. The flowers are small and pale-pink and white in color.

Green Bells of Ireland grows to three feet tall during the long Alaskan summer days. It is a wonderful addition to any garden.

Indications—living in the head instead of in the heart; weak connection between the physical body and the Earth; lacking a conscious heart connection to the natural world; unaware of the light and intelligence present in nature.

Healing Qualities—The essence of Green Bells of Ireland helps us make a conscious connection between our personal energy fields and the energy field of the planet.

This essence is helpful for all humans who have not yet made this connection, but it is especially useful for newborns who are being presented with their first opportunity to do so.

On a deeper level, Green Bells of Ireland helps us open our hearts and fine tune our perceptions to Earth frequencies of energy, enhancing our awareness of and communication with the intelligent, nonphysical light beings that inhabit the kingdoms of nature.

The degree of consciousness and awareness we embody with regard to our relationship with nature and the Earth is especially important for those who are living in crowded urban environments, where the naturally occurring plant, animal, and mineral communities have been greatly subdued, or in some cases completely removed.

In such cases, this essence can be used along with a practice of creative visualization and attunement to help individuals reconnect energetically with the energy of the natural world, and ground this connection into their daily lives.

I embrace my pain and fear with clarity and understanding.
My heart is filled with peace and serenity.

GREEN BOG ORCHID *Platanthera obtusata*

This tiny orchid occurs on short erect stems which grow from tuberous roots. The flowers are only 3/8 of an inch long and are quite transparent to light. Green Bog Orchid grows in damp or wet sites in woods and thickets throughout the southern two-thirds of Alaska. Its range extends southward into Canada and the northern United States.

Indications—attunement and sensitivity to the plant kingdom blocked by deeply held pain and fear; difficulty communicating from the heart; constricted energy flow in the heart chakra; lack of compassion for oneself and others.

Healing Qualities—Green Bog Orchid grows unobtrusively within the mat of vegetation that makes up its habitat. This orchid is so subtle that it requires a particularly focused quality of attention to sense its presence, and to connect with the vibration held within its physical form. Consequently, Green Bog Orchid is one of several Alaskan essences from green flowers that can help us develop a finely focused attunement and sensitivity to the plant kingdom.

This essence initiates and supports a profound cleansing and balancing process in the heart chakra. It is only through the release of blockages held in this energy center that an undeniably clear connection with nature can be established. This chakra is also where all core issues present within an individual need to be met with non-judgment and compassion. When we are in alignment with this flower's energy, we are able to journey into the heart and embrace these issues with clarity and understanding, and direct the healing energy that is available to where it is most needed.

The action of Green Bog Orchid is cyclic and self-perpetuating. As it catalyzes the release of pain and fear from the heart, a stronger current of love can enter, and one's subtle awareness and sensitivity to the nature kingdom is expanded. This perceptual expansion supports a further relaxation and opening of the heart, which in turn permits a deeper penetration by the essence.

The human and nature kingdoms are not separate. Any expansion of understanding and acceptance of self will be accompanied by a deeper awareness of nature. The essence of Green Bog Orchid is an important source of support for the development of our heart connection with nature, a connection that must be made within each of us if we are to fulfill our divine co-creative potential.

I surrender all inner conflict to the forces of Love.
In my heart I am One with all of creation.

GREEN FAIRY ORCHID *Hammarbya paludosa*

Green Fairy Orchid's tiny flowers occur on short, slender stems which rise from a cluster of two to four leaves.

This small, inconspicuous plant can be found growing in wet sphagnum bogs and muskegs from southcentral Alaska north to the Brooks Range.

Indications—defensiveness; attachment to separation; caught up in the dualities and contradictions of life; core imbalance between the masculine and feminine aspects of the self; difficulty communicating intimately from the heart; difficulty resolving conflicts within the heart.

Healing Qualities—The physical form of this flower is a subtle and miniature work of art, barely noticeable to the eye. But from within this tiny flower a powerful vortex of green energy radiates outward, beckoning to us with an important message. Green Fairy Orchid invites us to open our hearts and venture inward. It asks us to go deep within ourselves, into a realm beyond the mind and beyond the ego. It asks us to transcend our identification with the limited self and focus instead on the essential oneness we share with all life.

This flower essence helps us to know and accept oneness in our daily lives by guiding us on a special quest into the deepest realms of the heart—a journey to identify and release the dualities, contradictions, and conflicts that block our understanding and embodiment of the essential unity of the universe.

The major issue to be addressed on this journey is the state of imbalance that exists between our masculine and feminine energy. This balancing process needs to occur on an inner level within each individual before it can operate on an outer level between men and women. When masculine and feminine energies are held in extreme positions relative to each other, they are seen as opposites. Through an understanding of the key energetic principles of yin and yang, we learn that these are but two manifestations of the same energy, and that one cannot exist without the other.

The experience of knowing and mastering the fullness of the inner male and the inner female is a deep and profound process. The essence of Green Fairy Orchid is an important catalyst in this process, as it challenges us to come into total balance within ourselves, so that we may truly experience oneness in all aspects of our lives.

My energetic bond with the Earth is clear and strong.
All the nurturing and support I need is here, now.

GROVE SANDWORT *Moehringia lateriflora*

Grove Sandwort is a small, delicate flower with a worldwide presence. This member of the Pink family ranges from northwest U.S. across Canada, and around the globe to Siberia. It is found in woods, thickets, and dry meadows throughout Alaska.

Indications—weak connection to the Earth; difficulty adapting to new surroundings; bonding connections between mother and child lacking warmth and vitality; attempting to get emotional and physical nurturing from others in inappropriate ways; nursing problems in animals and humans.

Healing Qualities—This diminutive plant plays a vital role in the maintenance of life on this planet–that of strengthening the energetic bonds of communication between the Earth and her inhabitants.

In the woods, Grove Sandwort supports the well-being of plants growing nearby by helping them maintain a strong energetic connection with the Earth. Its essence may be used in the greenhouse and garden to help transplants stabilize themselves in their new locations. Within the animal kingdom, Grove Sandwort can be used in much the same way to help newborns establish a stronger connection with the Earth and with their new physical surroundings.

Grove Sandwort can also lend support to the evolving relationship of nurturing between mother and child, especially during the early part of the child's life when he or she is being nursed. This essence balances and aligns the mental and heart energies and can be used to help both mother and child communicate from their hearts rather than from their wills, particularly after either one has suffered some sort of emotional upheaval.

Grove Sandwort is also an important essence for adults who did not receive the quality or amount of nurturing they desired or deserved as children. Many will attempt to make up for this deficit by creating relationships based on the expectation that their partner will supply this missing energy. The essence of Grove Sandwort will help these individuals to instead create a connection with the feminine Earth forces, and from this bond receive the support and nurturance they need.

I open to the harmony that is inherent in Life.
I move through transitions with ease, grace, and
deep understanding.

HAIRY BUTTERWORT *Pinguicula villosa*

The delicate Hairy Butterwort flower is only 3/8 inch long, and is supported by a thin stem, rarely more than three inches tall, that is covered with long hairs. The leaves of this semi-carnivorous plant have special glands that secrete a greasy, sticky substance. Insects landing on these sticky areas become mired down and are held fast until digestion and absorption take place.

Hairy Butterwort may be found in peat bogs and around ponds in scattered locations throughout Alaska.

Indications—unable to acknowledge or trust in higher guidance and support, especially when confronted with a challenging situation or life lesson; lack of awareness of the issues that need to be resolved in a given situation; creating crisis or illness in order to move through a transformative process; learning one's lessons the hard way.

Healing Qualities—Throughout life there are moments of ascension, moments when we have truly completed a life lesson and by virtue of this are able to move through a threshold into a new state of consciousness.

The path we must travel to reach such a point of ascension is generally through the transformation of life patterns and habits that no longer contribute to our happiness or quality of life. In the more extreme cases, these patterns can manifest as physical illness, and we will find ourselves at a crossroads where we are challenged to learn the lessons at the core of each pattern and release the illness in the easiest way possible.

The key factors here are awareness, faith, and trust. All of us are accompanied throughout life by strong levels of spiritual guidance and support. If we are able to acknowledge, listen, and trust in this support, our learning experiences will be relatively smooth and gentle. Conversely, if we have a general lack of understanding of the issues that are needing to be resolved, and are not open to the help and guidance that is available to us, our growth processes can be stressful, chaotic, and crisis oriented.

This is where the essence of Hairy Butterwort is most applicable. It helps us expand our perceptions during difficult times so we can make a clear and conscious connection with the spiritual support and guidance that is available to us in each moment. Through this connection, we can access whatever assistance we need to move through any transformational process with balance, grace, and ease.

I receive all that I need through my love connection with
the Universe.
As I open my heart to others, unconditional love
flows through me.

HAREBELL *Campanula lasiocarpa*

Harebell is found in rocky alpine meadows and sandy tundra to at least 4,000 feet in the mountains throughout most of Alaska and northwestern Canada. It is a very small alpine plant, growing from two to four inches high; its leafy stem rising from a creeping rhizome. Each plant produces only one flower, which is bell shaped and quite large in relation to the rest of the plant. Harebells bloom in late July and August.

Indications—looking for love outside of oneself; believing that there is not enough love to go around; unable to receive the love that is available; difficulty sharing one's love because of not feeling loved by another.

Healing Qualities—Harebell speaks to us with power and clarity through its deep lilac-blue color and bell-shaped flowers. Its message is an invitation to open all areas of our life experience to Universal Love.

This essence asks us to redefine our perceptions about receiving love so that we may more clearly sense, feel, and embody the love that is available to us. Specifically, it helps us see more clearly into those areas where we are exerting control over, or manifesting resistance to, the acceptance of love. The primary belief Harebell questions is that love is only available from others and so there are many limitations to ever being able to receive the kind and amount of love that we need.

The Harebell essence teaches us to look within to find the love we seek, instead of looking for it outside of ourselves. Rather than focusing on the source of love as a limiting factor, we are challenged to look at and remove our own self-imposed mental and emotional limitations to receiving and giving forth the unlimited flow of love that is available to each of us.

The beautiful Harebell is a messenger of the joyous, living expression of Universal Love that is the basis for all life on this planet. Its essence can help us fully open our hearts to this life sustaining energy and allow it to move unconditionally through us to others.

I communicate clearly with the core of my being.
My awareness is constantly expanding into deeper contact
with all forms of life.

HORSETAIL *Equisetum arvense*

Horsetails are among the oldest plants, dating back to the pre-carboniferous period of 300 million years ago. Although today they may grow to six feet in height, horsetails, along with clubmoss, were tree-sized plants in that era.

Horsetail is a pioneer that can establish itself in areas that are not suitable for other plants, because it can grow in any soil. It occurs throughout of Alaska and is abundant in all parts of the world except in New Zealand and Australia.

Indications—difficulty communicating with others, including animals; distorted communication between the various levels of one's own consciousness; unable to contact the higher selves of others; imbalance between the rational and intuitive mind.

Healing Qualities—Horsetail is known for its ability to break rocks down into soil, a characteristic that emphasizes its role in the early days of our planet as a vibrational and evolutionary link between the mineral and plant kingdoms.

The essence of Horsetail highlights communication through connectedness. It is useful for people who want to expand their abilities to communicate on all levels and with all beings. It is of particular importance to those who need to communicate across cultural and ethnic boundaries, with people of different ages, and to those with differing degrees of education, understanding and life experience.

The unique gift of the Horsetail essence is that it reawakens and expands our ability to use a very ancient communication network, a system based on the fact that all living beings have fields of awareness. When these fields of awareness come in contact with each other, energy and information move between them.

Human beings lost contact with this network eons ago when we began to distrust one another and fear other forms of life. This led us to develop various levels of segregation and isolation which we employed as forms of protection. As this development continued, our conscious link with this living communications network continually weakened until most of us forgot it ever existed.

Horsetail helps us reconnect with this network by breaking down these old patterns of separation which we clearly do not need any more. Once these energies are released, our awareness is able to expand and reconnect with other fields of awareness, facilitating an increased level of communication with ourselves, each other, and with all members of our Earth family.

I am a radiant spiritual being.
My spiritual power constantly shines outward into all
aspects of my life.

ICELANDIC POPPY *Papaver nudicaule*

Icelandic Poppy is a hardy perennial that can be an excellent addition to any garden. The brightly colored flowers are displayed in orange, yellow, red, pink and white. They are miniature solar collectors and one often finds small insects "sunbathing" within the protective floral cup.

Poppy plants are distinguished by the black hairs covering the leaves, stems, and calyces. The single flower buds droop as they develop on the lengthening stem. As the flower opens and becomes upright, the two halves of the calyx fall from the plant and the once tightly compacted flowers unfold like wrinkled silk.

Icelandic Poppies can also be found along roadsides and in waste places in the interior of the state where they have escaped cultivation.

Indications—keeping to oneself; holding one's light and radiance inside; tenuous sense of spiritual identity; lack of spiritual energy in the lower chakras; weak connection to one's spiritual or angelic self.

Healing Qualities—On clear days, these brightly colored flowers turn their faces to follow the sun as it circumnavigates the summer sky. This delicate sensitivity to the heat and power of the sun is a physical symbol of the healing power of this poppy essence–to support the gentle unfoldment of spiritual receptivity and radiance.

This essence facilitates spiritual development by helping us remain consistently open to the universal qualities of intelligence and wisdom that are inherently present in each of us.

Icelandic Poppy is helpful for people who have a high degree of spiritual awareness and development, but who are hesitant to let their light shine out into the world where others can see it. These flowers teach us that sharing our inner light with the world is one of the most powerful ways to strengthen the flow of spiritual energy coming through our bodies.

This essence is also important for those who are caught up in dramatic and confusing situations in their lives, and who feel they have lost touch with their sources of guidance and higher wisdom. In this context, the essence of Icelandic Poppy can be used to help reestablish a strong inner spiritual focus that will help them find their way back to the truth of who they really are.

I open my mind to pure knowing.
I easily receive the wisdom that is available to me in this moment.

JACOB'S LADDER *Polemonium pulcherrimum*

Jacob's Ladder is one of the hardiest wildflowers growing in the interior of Alaska. It starts blooming immediately after the snow leaves the ground and continues to flower in many areas until late August.

The common name of this plant is derived from the numerous leaflets, resembling rungs of a ladder, which grow from erect stems two to twelve inches high. Flowers are born in a cluster, and are lavender-blue contrasting with a vivid orange-yellow ring at the base of the flower cup.

Indications—obsessive thinking; attempting to mentally control and manipulate life in order to fulfill one's needs and desires; believing that unless one is in control, one will never receive life's necessities; trying to anticipate all possible outcomes before taking action; lacking trust in the spiritual world.

Healing Qualities—This essence is for those who feel they must maintain a constant mental vigilance, who find themselves laying awake at night obsessively worrying about the details of their lives. This hyper-vigilance creates high levels of tension in the body, and can lead to conditions such as insomnia.

Jacob's Ladder brings relief to such persons by addressing the issue of mental manipulation. When a person is convinced that they must manipulate life to insure happiness and fulfillment, their days will be characterized by struggle, and they risk being manipulated by others. Ironically, in their attempts to maintain control over the hundreds of daily interactions in their life, they often end up creating the kinds of experiences they fear out of their resistance towards them.

The essence of Jacob's Ladder helps us create a union between the mental and spiritual realms that is based on a discipline of acceptance rather than on control and manipulation. It helps us shift our mental focus from constantly trying to figure things out, to opening to receive what is available in each moment.

This essence also helps us examine the relationship between our intentions, motivations, and desires. As our awareness of this relationship grows, we are better able to align our emotional and mental capacities with the creative impulses of the soul. It is through such a co-creative connection with our higher selves that we are able to manifest all that is necessary to lead a happy and fulfilling life.

I am fully centered in my body in this moment.
I welcome true balance into all areas of my life.

LABRADOR TEA *Ledum palustre*

Labrador Tea is a many branched, resinous evergreen shrub growing one to four feet tall. Its flowers are numerous and conspicuously fragrant, occurring in clusters at the tips of twigs. Its fruits mature in July and August and are present most of the winter.

Labrador Tea is common in black spruce and birch forest bogs. It establishes itself abundantly after a fire in the spruce habitat.

Indications—addictions; attempting to balance one extreme with another; instability during emotional catharsis; lack of unity between the physical, emotional, and mental levels of being; difficulty coming back to center after a traumatic or unsettling experience; extreme imbalance in any area of one's life.

Healing Qualities—Labrador Tea helps us move from an unbalanced, transitional state to a centered, energized one. It works with us to calm and center extreme imbalances of physical, emotional, and mental energy, and helps us integrate these different flows of energy so they may function in the body in a unified way.

This essence is especially effective in times of emotional catharsis or after a traumatic experience, as its powerful vibration can bring a balancing and centering influence to any situation we are involved in.

Labrador Tea is particularly helpful for those who, throughout their lives, have attempted to balance one extreme with another. A common example is overwork and the habitual use of addictive substances, such as coffee, tobacco, and alcohol. It is difficult for some to stop using such substances because they bring a sense of equilibrium which these individuals can no longer achieve by themselves. To make matters worse, this feeling of stability is temporary. Attempts to maintain it over time require increasing amounts of the addictive substances, which lead to deeper levels of instability.

If such persons wish to reverse these kinds of habitual patterns, it may be necessary for them to work with this essence over an extended period of time, so it will have the opportunity to move through and bring harmony to all areas of their lives. When used in this context, Labrador Tea will first work to open an individual's awareness to the fact that a particular imbalance exists. It will then support them in making the necessary mental, emotional, and physical adjustments that are required to bring each aspect of their life back into balance.

My actions are grounded in integrity and humility.
I recognize my individual contribution
to the evolution of humanity.

LACE FLOWER *Tiarella trifoliata*

Lace Flower is a delicate woodland member of the saxifrage family. Its genus name, Tiarella, translates as "coronet" and refers to the crown worn by princes and princesses. Lace Flower's blossoms, so often overlooked due to their small size, are indeed as lovely as any sovereign's coronet. The species name, trifoliata, refers to the three leaves present on each stem.

Indications—feeling insignificant and unsure of how one's personal or professional contributions fit into the whole; lacking self-awareness and self-appreciation; unable to see one's own natural beauty and intrinsic value.

Healing Qualities—The simplest plant, insect, or mineral are all marvels of creation, adding significance to the whole. Even though their roles may not be obvious, their impact may be great indeed.

People may feel they are insignificant because their work is in the home or in small towns or out-of-the-way places. Yet we are all important, as the essence of Lace Flower reminds us. No matter where we are, we can do whatever we do with love and awareness, and the impact of this can radiate outward in countless ways.

The essence of Lace Flower is especially helpful for those who have issues of extreme low self esteem and self-worth. These issues can arise from being the victim of cultural bias and prejudice, favoritism at work, or from the experience of being dominated by a member of one's family. Lace Flower enables individuals who have had these kinds of life experiences to get back in touch with the true core of their inner worth and from this place express their unique talents and abilities with grace, poise, and humility.

This tiny, delicate, and regal flower, growing in the shade of giant spruce trees, reminds us that our true importance is not based on whether we are seen, but on the quality of our expression. It encourages us to base our value on the integrity of our actions and our belief in ourselves rather than on artificial and capricious methods of approval.

I release all trauma; in its place, I welcome harmony and balance.
I now move deeply within to reconnect with my soul's
purpose in this lifetime.

LADIES' TRESSES *Spiranthes romanzoffiana*

This beautiful plant has small, faintly perfumed flowers that are closely packed in three spiral ranks, like neatly braided hair. They grow on an unbranched stem which may reach a height of 12 inches. Ladies' Tresses' range is extensive, occurring in moist places in fields, swamps, and alpine areas up to 3,000 feet throughout most of the state of Alaska.

Indications—lacking enthusiasm; prone to procrastination; little or no awareness of life purpose or life orientation; difficulty seeing or understanding the connection between one's life lessons and one's life purpose; having a hard time getting interested or involved with life after a serious injury or traumatic experience.

Healing Qualities—Each one of us begins the process of physical incarnation with a certain amount of conscious awareness of our goals for this lifetime, and of the lessons we have chosen to promote the realization of these goals. This information is part of the original archetype or energy blueprint of each individual and is available after birth at the cellular level of consciousness.

During the gestation period, birth, and early months of life, a certain amount of this awareness can be lost or forgotten. Some of this loss is necessary, in order that the lessons may be learned in the way and to the degree necessary. However, if these sensitive periods are characterized by extremely painful or traumatic experiences, then the majority of a person's awareness of life direction and purpose can become unavailable to the conscious mind.

In such cases, a long period of adjustment and healing may be required before an individual can once again become fully aligned with their soul forces and move forward along a chosen path. This adjustment period can generally be characterized by chronic problems with specific areas of the body, problems that logically reflect the trauma that is still present.

Ladies' Tresses is a key essence for the release of such deeply held trauma. It is able to gently penetrate into the core of one's being to catalyze the release of painful energies that have collected at the cellular level. As this traumatic energy is released, information pertaining to the individual's life purpose once again becomes available. This essence then helps the conscious mind understand and integrate this information, so that it can be used to create new thought and life-style patterns which will encourage a more thorough and efficient alignment of the physical being with its highest spiritual potential.

My awareness opens to what was once invisible to me.
My energy system is vibrant, focused, and
responsive to my needs.

LADY'S SLIPPER *Cypripedium guttatum*

Lady's Slipper is a rare, attractive orchid with distinctive features. The floral stem rises from a slender rootstock at the center of two lance shaped leaves, and bears one flower that is subtended by a single bract.

The flower itself is highly modified with a brightly colored pouch, overhanging lid, and two lateral petals. The flower's color is variable depending on location but it is generally pink or white; the pouch being dotted with purple or greenish-purple blotches.

This species of Lady's Slipper is found in meadows and open mossy woods in southeastern, southcentral, and interior Alaska.

Indications—resistance to receiving healing energy from others; lacking sensitivity to the flow of energy in and around one's body; unbalanced flow of energies between the chakras, along the spine, and within the central nervous system; weak central vertical axis.

Healing Qualities—This Lady's Slipper orchid is a well-hidden forest dweller. It requires us to come to a place of inner quiet and attunement before it will reveal itself.

The energy surrounding and infusing Lady's Slipper is highly concentrated. Its essence helps us focus, circulate, and balance the energy flows in and around our bodies, and direct additional energy to those areas that have been depleted and are in need of regeneration and renewal.

Lady's Slipper works specifically with the major energy pathways in the body–the chakras, the central nervous system, and particularly the large nerve pathways that run along the spine.

This essence not only helps us balance and regulate the flow of energy along these pathways, but at the same time helps us increase our awareness and sensitivity to them, so that we can learn to focus and direct our life energies more efficiently.

Lady's Slipper can be helpful to both client and practitioner when introduced into an energetic healing session. The therapist can use this essence to become more attuned to the client's energy flow, specifically to those areas that are in need of healing. This essence can also be used when the client needs a gentle catalyst that will help them open to receive the healing energy that is being offered by the therapist.

My mind is Light, my heart is Light, there is no separation.
I open my mind to the wisdom of my heart.

LAMB'S QUARTERS *Chenopodium album*

Lamb's Quarters is an introduced herb, now common along the banks of streams, near settlements, and in gardens. It is considered to be one of the best tasting wild edible plants in the state.

Lamb's Quarters grows in a branching upright mode, generally reaching a height of two to three feet. Its leaves are triangular or oval in shape, and are green on top and pale green underneath. The tiny flowers are clustered in dense spikes near the top of the stems.

Indications—mental inflexibility; blocked intuition; perspective limited to what one can understand or "figure out" with the mind; lacking balance and harmony between the mind and heart; mind always attempting to interpret and rationalize what the heart feels.

Healing Qualities—This essence is for those who are highly intellectual, and who operate primarily from a rational perspective. It is helpful for those who have a very confrontational mind, a mind that is closely connected to the ego and threatened by information that comes from anywhere else but itself.

A state of mind where the rational is over-emphasized limits an individual to one way of thinking and keeps the mental processes from being able to come into harmony with higher levels of perception. A person with this mental orientation, when challenged with a problem, will be limited by the amount of information that is available for a solution.

The essence of Lamb's Quarters helps the mind connect with additional sources of information by clearing and expanding the channel of communication between the heart and mind. As this channel is opened, information from the body, the environment, and higher sources of inspiration can enter into the equation.

This essence encourages the flowering of a softer and more heart centered mental perspective, a less confrontational attitude that empowers the mind to accept and use all the relevant information and wisdom that is available to it, regardless of the source.

I am aware of my own Divine nature.
I relate to the world with fearlessness.

MONKSHOOD *Aconitum delphinifolium*

Monkshood is a radiant beacon in the forest. The flowers are a deep blue or purple, or in rare cases white. They are most easily recognized by the characteristic monk-like hood on top. The species name for this plant is derived from its similarity in form to the wild delphinium flowers and leaves. All parts of the Monkshood plant are poisonous, especially the seeds and tubers which contain the highly toxic alkaloids aconitine and aconine.

Monkshood grows throughout the interior of Alaska in birch forests and meadows, and in alpine tundra and arctic slope habitats.

Indications—weighed down by inner burdens; fearful of sharing one's private self with others; weak boundaries; difficulty being in close physical proximity to others, especially in situations of intense conflict; avoidance of deep emotional contact with others.

Healing Qualities—The Monkshood essence is for sensitive individuals who feel repulsed by others, who cannot allow true physical or emotional access because they lack well-defined energetic boundaries, and for those who do not realize the effect their energy has on others.

This plant has a very strong energy field and incredibly well-defined boundaries. Its essence can be used to greatly improve the strength and delineation of our energy boundaries. Once we have this sense of protection in our auras, we can use the Monkshood essence to help us create a protected inner space that is insulated from the conflicts of the outside world.

The presence of this sacred inner space, which is similar to what one would encounter in a monastery, helps us to get in touch with deeper levels of ourselves, aspects that were previously beneath our conscious comprehension. As we continue on this protected journey, we come face to face with the power and presence of the Divine nature that we hold within.

This awareness of our inner divinity enables us to project a stronger sense of our true spiritual identity out into the world. We are empowered to let go of our inner burdens, drop the heaviness from our hearts, and relate to the world with fearlessness.

I nurture myself and all beings placed in my care
with love and sensitivity.
I create beauty and harmony through celebration and play.

MOSCHATEL *Adoxa moschatelina*

Moschatel flowers grow in geometric cubes. These are composed of four blossoms on each side of the stem, and one at the top. Each flower has four petals with a whorl of stamens and anthers on the inside. The whole inflorescence is green except for the anthers and pollen which have a yellowish tint.

This delicate perennial herb grows in moist woods, thickets, and meadows throughout much of Alaska south of the Brooks Range.

Indications—workaholic; trying too hard; believing that everything must come through struggle; worried and concerned about others; unsure of how to nurture oneself and other living beings.

Healing Qualities—Moschatel plants play an important role in the maintenance and development of the other plants that grow in close proximity to them. This is especially true when Moschatel grows next to a garden, where it harmonizes the different energies that are present, and generates additional energy to fill in the areas where there is a lack of life force. This provides a more continuous energy pattern for the whole garden, making it more resistant to insects and disease. This helpful vibration can be introduced into a garden even when this plant is not available by adding the Moschatel essence to the watering system on an ongoing basis.

Moschatel is also an important essence for those who would like to cultivate an ongoing, conscious partnership with nature. It helps us develop our sensitivities to the plant kingdom so that we can learn how to promote the growth and development of plants in a more enjoyable way. It does this by opening our awareness to how the elemental beings nurture the plants they have been given responsibility for, and that is through play–a celebration of life that is constantly weaving the energies of Earth and spirit into perfect harmony. Moschatel brings us a reminder from the elemental kingdom that everything we humans could possibly need can also be realized through this playful celebration of life.

We cannot live a healthy and balanced life unless we learn to fulfill our needs in ways that are fun and enjoyable. Our skill in caring for other forms of life will grow as we learn to create our own physical and spiritual harmony through celebration and play, rather than through overwork and worry.

I allow healing grace to flow forth unconditionally.
I fully and freely forgive; my highest good
now appears in perfect form.

MOUNTAIN WORMWOOD *Artemisia tilesii*

The Artemisia genus honors Artemis, the Greek moon goddess who considered wormwood a sacred herb. Worldwide, there are about two hundred Artemisia species. Common names range from wormwood, derived from the plant's use as a vermifuge or "wormer", to sagebrush, from its use as a spice; stinkweed, due to its aromatic qualities, and caribou leaves, from caribou browsing the leaves. Its range extends from the Arctic to Africa, with the majority of species being concentrated in the Northern hemisphere.

Indications—unresolved anger and resentment; holding grudges against those who we feel have caused us hurt or pain; feeling disappointed with oneself or others; cannot easily forgive the self or others for past actions regardless of the intent behind them.

Healing Qualities—As an herbal remedy, *Artemisia tilesii* is widely used by Native Alaskans throughout the state. Externally, it can be applied as a poultice or herbal oil for aches and pains, sprains and strains. Internally, wormwood tincture is excellent for stresses ranging from jet lag to cold symptoms.

As a flower essence, Mountain Wormwood works with the quality of forgiveness. Sometimes we hold anger, disappointment, or grudges within ourselves. Perhaps a partner left us suddenly. Maybe a parent or teacher belittled us or physically abused us. These emotional wounds, though not visible as physical scars, can continue to affect our lives.

For these unforgiven areas, Mountain Wormwood is the essence of choice. It helps us eliminate the "worms of discontent" that erode our peace of mind, clears our consciousness of past resentments, and encourages us to allow all of our judgments to dissolve. As we focus on love and compassion, healing occurs. We are then able to bring all of our relationships into balance, and live freely and fully in the present moment.

It is safe enough for me to incarnate now.
My being is surrounded with infinite gentleness;
I am caressed and nurtured into wholeness.

NORTHERN LADY'S SLIPPER *Cypripedium passerinum*

Northern Lady's Slipper is a very fragrant and beautiful plant. Its solitary flowers with short, greenish sepals and whitish petals have an egg-shaped "pouch". This pouch is about 3/4" long and is white or pale magenta with bright purple spots on the interior wall that sometimes show faintly through to the outside. This orchid is found throughout the central interior of Alaska, blooming in late June or early July in bogs, gravel washes and wet talus.

Indications—disincarnate; weak body/soul connection; traumatic birth experience; pain and trauma held very deeply in the body; resistance to receiving healing energy; feeling unsupported by life.

Healing Qualities—This essence is a very powerful catalyst to use during any kind of conscious healing activity, especially when the focus is to touch and heal a trauma from the past that is being held very deeply within the physical and energetic structure of the body. A prime example is the trauma one can experience when the body and spirit become partially separated at some point in time leading up to, during, or shortly after birth.

This disconnection often happens when the incarnating spirit feels a lack of physical and energetic support during the gestation period and birth process, and as a result resists becoming fully incarnated. Most individuals will maintain this resistance until they feel a level of physical safety that encourages them to complete the process of incarnating onto the physical plane. Northern Lady's Slipper facilitates the restoration of this vital body/spirit connection by supplying a very gentle, yet penetrative quality of energetic support. This gentle, loving energy helps a person begin the process of releasing the many layers of pain and tension that have accumulated around the initial trauma.

These layers of energy must be cleared before the body/spirit connection can be fully restored, and the process of their removal can often be slow and painful. Northern Lady's Slipper is valuable in that it can help people let go of successive layers of pain and trauma without them having to consciously reexperience each one as it is being released.

This essence is a positive catalyst for adults of any age who are involved with healing the unresolved traumas of their inner child. It can also be helpful for those who are just beginning life on the physical plane. The essence can be added to the baby's bath water as soon as possible after the birth and given as needed during the early days and months of life.

My perceptions are drenched with reality.
I believe what I see.

NORTHERN TWAYBLADE *Listera borealis*

This delicate member of the Orchid family occurs in moist woods and muskegs throughout much of Alaska. Its tiny flowers occur in small numbers on straight green stems that are tended by two opposing leaves.

Indications—spiritual awareness blocked by fear and resistance; unaware of the subtler aspects of one's own consciousness and of the spiritual consciousness that is present in nature; unable to make practical use of one's sensitivities; having difficulty sharing one's inner experiences with others.

Healing Qualities—The Northern Twayblade essence works on a very deep level within the heart to cleanse and release blockages that limit an individual's ability to perceive and experience subtle levels of energy. This essence is especially helpful for those who are committed to a path of working with the kingdoms of nature on a very deep and profound level. It is also helpful for anyone who wants to integrate the finer, subtler energies of spirit into the denser, more physical aspects of life on Earth.

This essence can work in two ways. If a person who is well grounded and comfortable in the physical world wants to develop an attunement to the subtle realms of nature, then this essence could be used to increase their perception of the subtler aspects of their own consciousness. With continued practice, they would then be able to expand the range of their sensitivities to include an awareness of the spiritual consciousness that resides within all of nature.

On the other hand, if an individual already possesses a sensitivity to the subtler realms, then the Northern Twayblade essence could be used to help them ground this attunement more fully into the physical body and physical experience.

In either case, the Northern Twayblade essence works by catalyzing the release of fear and resistance from deep levels of the heart. This helps the individual prepare and maintain a place where the subtle and spiritual can work together in an increasingly harmonious partnership with the physical. Such a partnership is absolutely necessary if we are to come to the deepest possible understanding of how all physical manifestation is truly a manifestation of the Divine.

My energy attracts people and situations that support
my highest good.
I act with full awareness and consideration
of my impact on others.

ONE-SIDED WINTERGREEN *Pyrola secunda*

One-Sided Wintergreen is a low evergreen plant with yellowish-green leaves. One of the most distinguishing characteristics of this easily recognizable plant are the small bell-shaped flowers that are all borne along one side of the slightly curved stem.

One-Sided Wintergreen is a common plant in moist thickets and woodlands throughout southcentral, eastern, and interior Alaska. It blooms from late June to early August.

Indications—lack of definition to one's energy field; strongly influenced by other people's energy; constantly attracting people and situations that are not in harmony with one's true self; unaware of how one's actions and energy affect others.

Healing Qualities—The essence of One-Sided Wintergreen helps us create and maintain functional energy boundaries that are in alignment with our highest truth and life purpose. This plant holds the archetype of physical embodiment in perfect harmony with spirit. Its flowers can help us learn how to define our self-expression in such a way as to attract people and situations that will help us carry out the work that we are here to do.

The flowers of One-Sided Wintergreen show us how we can exist in close physical proximity to others and still maintain the integrity of our own energy field. They do this by expanding our awareness of resonance, which is the naturally occurring exchange of energy between two objects. Through an understanding of this principle, we can become more sensitized as to how our actions and energies affect others, and how we in turn are affected by the energies and actions of others.

The lesson of this essence is that it is not necessary to identify with the energy patterns of others in order to maintain our own boundaries. Instead, we are asked to focus on the quality of energy that we are projecting outward to others. This projection will determine the quality of energy, and therefore the kinds of people, that we will attract. If we strongly project the truth of who we are, we will attract people and situations that support this truth, making it easier for us to function in the physical world in alignment with our Divine purpose.

In the midst of intense activity, I am at rest.
I go forward into this day in perfect balance.

OPIUM POPPY *Papaver commutatum*

With its brilliant red fringes enveloping a pure white center, this variety of poppy can be a very eye catching addition to any garden. The Opium Poppy flower essence was prepared as a sun-infusion in a co-creative garden near Homer, Alaska.

Indications—addicted to expansion; unable to find a balance point between activity and rest; deep exhaustion; living in the future; unaware of one's past accomplishments; difficulty understanding and integrating lessons and experiences.

Healing Qualities—Humans have long expressed the imbalance of extremes. A derivative of the Opium Poppy can lead us into extreme imbalance and separation from the body when used in drug form, but the subtler energies of the flower essence offer us a new archetype for balance within human form.

This essence helps us establish a point of balance between doing and being. The white center of the flower is the Zen space–the fiery red fringes, the energetic dance of evolution. Together these symbolize a balanced play of soul activation and peaceful surrender.

The Opium Poppy essence works with us to create a peaceful and neutral space within where we may truthfully and consistently acknowledge and integrate the steps we are taking in our evolutionary journey. If we do not have this level of integration operating in our lives, we will eventually create an accumulation of unacknowledged experience and information. This backlog can motivate us to achieve more and more simply because we do not have a clear understanding of what it is we have already accomplished.

The essence of Opium Poppy can be used to help us process this backlog, allowing us to proceed in life with a motivation that is based on a clear and full understanding of our life experience.

The Opium Poppy essence gives us the opportunity to update ourselves to the present, to live directly in this moment. The healing this essence offers is the lasting establishment of a point of balance between evolution and being, with each new level of balance we achieve becoming the foundation for new growth and experience.

I am actively connected to the deepest levels of my true self.
I follow my life's path with calm determination.

PAPER BIRCH *Betula papyrifera*

Paper Birch grows 20 to 80 feet in height and four to 20 inches in trunk diameter. It is common throughout the Alaskan interior up to tree line.

Paper Birch is easily identified by its smooth white or pinkish bark which peels off in thin, paper like strips. It is usually found in a mixture of white or black spruce which replaces it in the successional sequence after a fire.

Even though it is continually peeling off in thin sheets, the bark of paper birch is highly resistant to weathering. Downed trees may rot away, leaving an intact tube of bark. When building sod-roofed cabins, people sometimes put durable birch-bark sheeting under the sod to provide some waterproofing.

Birch catkins bloom in the spring from buds that are formed during the previous summer, fall, and winter.

Indications—difficulty making decisions that affect our life direction; unsure of where we are on our path; no continuity to our actions; lacking the determination to reach goals once they have been identified; doing what others want us to do, rather than what we want to do.

Healing Qualities—The positive qualities supported by the Paper Birch essence are calm determination, a steady awareness of purpose, and a continuity of focus that comes from a clear and active connection with deeper levels of the self.

This essence is useful whenever we face important life decisions, feel that we should do something but don't have the enthusiasm for it, or are feeling lost and unsure about the path of action we are pursuing and whether it will serve our highest good.

Paper Birch helps us gain a fresh perspective on what we are doing with our lives. It supports a process of realignment with our life purpose by helping us get back in touch with the underlying true and essential self that is present within us. This true self is often obscured by an accumulated mass of outdated thoughts and old programing, as well as tension, fear, and anxiety. The Paper Birch essence introduces a calming, clarifying, and relaxing energy that helps us move our focus from these chaotic thoughts and confusing emotions to the peace and joy that are present at core levels of our being. From this place of calm awareness we are better able to make key life decisions that support the truth of who we are.

I greet the Earth with each step that I take.
I walk through this life with balance and grace.

PINEAPPLE WEED *Matricaria matricariodes*

Pineapple Weed is a common wild ground-cover characterized by feathery leaves and rayless, pineapple-scented flowers. Alaskans commonly refer to this sun-loving plant as wild chamomile.

Like its relative, German Chamomile (*Matricaria chamomilla*), this plant is a traditional remedy for easing pains of childbirth and for soothing colicky babies. The genus name stems from either mater (meaning mother) or matrix (meaning womb).

Indications—disconnected from the Earth; accident prone; lack of harmony with one's physical environment; unaware of the support and nurturing that is available from nature; weak nurturing bond between mother and child.

Healing Qualities— Healing herbs often grow in large quantities in close proximity to those who have need of them. Pineapple Weed grows abundantly near homes and in areas frequently trampled by children, such as school yards and playgrounds.

The essence of Pineapple Weed is excellent for young, active children and adults of any age who are participating in sports. It encourages a calm awareness of one's body, and can be used to assist anyone in gaining freedom from injury and risk by helping them harmonize their energies with their physical surroundings.

The Pineapple Weed essence works by connecting and harmonizing one's body consciousness with the consciousness of the Earth. It improves grounding by increasing our awareness of our legs and feet and their energetic relationship with the planet. This additional awareness also results in improved circulation in those parts of the body.

Pineapple Weed is also useful for older people who are starting to have difficulty walking by themselves, or are prone to accidents. Mothers and mothers-to-be may also experience feelings of well-being and peacefulness with this essence, helping them to better cope with the demands of pregnancy and parenting.

I celebrate life with courage and openness.
I am nourished by the beauty that surrounds me.

PRICKLY WILD ROSE *Rosa acicularis*

Prickly Wild Rose grows as a spiny multi-branched shrub one to four feet high. The flowers are composed of a greenish base of five narrow leaflike sepals and five pink to rose colored petals.

This rose flowers from June to July and the fruits or rose hips become ripe in August and September. Rose hips supply the richest source of Vitamin C in this region, retaining a large percentage of their vitamin content even after being cooked or dried. Prickly Wild Rose is common in the shaded under-growth of deciduous and spruce forests and in thickets along roadsides throughout Alaska.

Indications—disinterested in life; apathetic; feeling hopeless; lacking trust and faith in oneself and in others; retreats into self when faced with painful situations in life; unable to keep one's heart open when involved in a conflict; not feeling safe or secure enough to remain open to others.

Healing Qualities—The physical characteristics of Prickly Wild Rose offer us a visually descriptive representation of its vibrational healing qualities.

The flowers exist in a state of openness and vulnerability–their petals are easily loosened from the base of the sepals. They beckon to us with their beauty, invoking in us a sense of interest and wonder. The thorny branches give protection to these delicate flowers so that they may evolve into the fruiting stage of the nourishing rose hip.

The Prickly Wild Rose essence helps us manifest and maintain an aura of openness and courageous interest in life in the face of seemingly adverse circumstances. From such openness and faith comes a sense of calm and the knowledge that we will continue to blossom and bring our hopes to fruition.

This essence is particularly helpful for those who have become disinterested in life because of what they perceived were past failures and lost opportunities. These feelings seem to surface more often as we get older, especially when we go through what is called the mid-life crisis. The sense is that we haven't been able to do what we wanted to do in our lives, and we wonder if we ever will.

For these situations, or any important life transition, the essence of Prickly Wild Rose can be of assistance. It can help us let go of past difficulties, look at our challenges and accomplishments honestly, and look forward to the future with joy, optimism, and excitement.

I welcome the flood waters of transformation.
I am cleansed, I am free, I live this day with glee.

RIVER BEAUTY *Epilobium latifolium*

River Beauty is a shorter but showier fireweed species, common on the banks of rivers and streams. It often sprouts to life after floods have rearranged riverbeds. The genus name, *Epilobium*, translates as "upon the pod" and refers to the long seedpods that form in late summer. These pods release copious amounts of seeds that are carried on the wind by downy parachutes, enabling the regenerative efforts of the plant to continue.

Indications—shock and trauma from emotional or sexual abuse; shock and trauma in animals; unable to regain emotional balance after an accident or catastrophic event, especially those involving the loss of life and property; physical tightness and tension resulting from unexpressed grief and sadness.

Healing Qualities—Like the field fireweed that helps the soil regenerate after a fire, River Beauty renews the land after a flood. Floods are symbolic of great cleansing and radical change. Perhaps you have experienced a "washing away" of a relationship or job. Maybe there was a tragedy in the family or the passing away of a close friend. The River Beauty essence helps soothe the effects of such traumatic events, and supports the necessary process of emotional reorientation and recovery one must go through after the shock from such an experience has passed.

This essence also empowers us to work with intense emotional energy, especially when it has been repressed in the physical body. When we are in the middle of an emergency, we usually don't take the time to check into our emotions. We put our feelings aside and just deal with what is in front of us. While this may help us get through the situation, it is important that we eventually acknowledge how we are feeling and process those emotions that are present. River Beauty expands our awareness of where we are holding powerful emotional energies, such as grief and sadness, in our bodies. It then helps us exchange them for the clear and vibrant energy of nature. In the same way, this essence encourages us to surrender our emotional attachment to that which has been lost in years past.

River Beauty is an appropriate essence for the current age, when the Earth and her inhabitants are undergoing many dramatic changes. This essence helps us to see adverse circumstances as potential for cleansing and growth, and realize that as the old is washed away, we are given the opportunity to create new experiences full of beauty and joy.

As I release my attachment to the known,
I move closer to true knowing.
I surrender my will to the Highest and reunite with the
Source of all Life.

ROUND-LEAVED SUNDEW *Drosera rotundifolia*

Round-Leaved Sundew is one of fifty or so insectivorous plants world-wide. Its leaves are edged with highly modified hairs, each tipped by a drop of sticky fluid. This is a trap for insects, which supplement the diet of the plant with phosphorus and nitrogen compounds, essential elements not readily picked up by the roots from their watery and acidic surroundings.

Small, white flowers with four to five petals are born on leafless stalks that bend over with the weight of the blossoms.

Indications—stubbornness; attachment to the known; fearful of the unknown; resistance to growth and transformation; would rather struggle than change; over identification with the ego; lack of communication between the higher and lower self.

Healing Qualities—The essence of Round-Leaved Sundew supports the release of inappropriate ego attachment to the past.

The human ego has within its makeup a stubborn and tenacious ability to hold on and survive, whatever the circumstances. It is this perseverance which enables the soul to make its journey through the difficulties and challenges of physical life. However, if this ego tenacity manifests as an unwillingness to grow and change, then it becomes a barrier to the soul's evolution.

Whenever a person is attempting to evolve to a new level of consciousness, there will be a time when they will be asked to surrender their ego attachment to the known and venture into the unknown. What the individual is actually being asked to do, is surrender a part of their identification with the limited self and identify instead with the unlimited source of their being.

The ego is a part of the human being that is necessary for survival in this dimension. Our task is not to diminish the ego, but rather to give it appropriate acknowledgment and support. This essence teaches us how to bring the strength and tenacity of the ego into harmony and balance with the wisdom and guidance of the higher self. Then they can function together and bring us ever closer to our reunification with the source of all life.

I open my heart to the Source of my being;
I know why I am here.
I am a child of the universe; I feel welcome wherever I go.

SHOOTING STAR *Dodecatheon frigidum*

This northern species of Shooting Star is found in wet alpine meadows, moist tundra, heathlands, and open forest throughout much of Alaska except in the extreme northern and southern coastal areas.

Its bright nodding flowers rise to heights of 12" to 16" from a cluster of smooth, deep green leaves. They generally bloom from mid-June to late July.

Indications—pain and trauma resulting from a difficult birth experience; sense of not belonging on the Earth; homesickness for a place one cannot identify; unable to consciously understand why one is here; doesn't feel support for being on the Earth; difficulty tuning into inner spiritual guidance.

Healing Qualities—The essence of this graceful flower assists those who need to develop a clear sense of their purpose on Earth and a practical understanding of how best to fulfill that purpose.

This variety of Shooting Star grows high up in the mountains, far away from humans and their habitations. Its essence is particularly helpful when a person feels they don't fit into their earthly surroundings–when they feel alienated, unwanted, or homesick for a place they can't identify.

Shooting Star strengthens a person's innate ability to connect with levels of guidance and information that will help them understand the larger context of their situation on Earth. This awareness empowers them to make the inner adjustments they need in order to feel more welcome on the planet.

Shooting Star is often indicated for those who have had a difficult birth, and can be a catalyst for the removal of pain and trauma remaining in the body from the birth experience. It is also helpful for those who have been involved in programs of personal growth and healing for some time and have a conscious understanding regarding their true purpose in life, but want to apply this knowledge in a new or more direct and effective way.

In this context, the essence is best used in an ongoing meditation or attunement program that is designed to develop one's connections with inner spiritual guidance. The prolonged use of Shooting Star in such a program will bring the individual into contact with information that can be used over time to assist them in making their journey through life easier and more fruitful.

There is an immense amount of loving support available to assist each of us during our sojourn on the Earth, and the essence of Shooting Star is offered to help us connect with that support in ever-increasing ways.

I am one with omnipresent light.
I am eternally linked to the light of my soul family.

SINGLE DELIGHT *Moneses uniflora*

Single Delight is a unique looking plant that resides in moist forest soils in shady wooded areas throughout Alaska. Its single white flower towers three inches above the ground, looking downward as if to illuminate all things below. This growth habit inspires other common names like Frog's Reading Light and Shy Maiden.

Indications—feeling isolated and alone, especially during a dark or depressing time; sadness after moving and leaving friends behind; unable to sense or feel the connection with one's soul family.

Healing Qualities—This plant prefers to grow in areas that are sheltered from the sun and its single white blossom points not to the sky but straight down towards the ground. When one catches a glimpse of a Single Delight flower in a shady forest glen, it appears to glow with its own inner light. This signature suggests a strong connection to lunar, rather than solar forces, and symbolizes the power of light that shines in darkness.

Single Delight is for those who feel alone and separate, who are trying to find a connection with others through the perceived darkness and isolation of their present experience. This essence teaches us that these feelings of separation can be healed by opening our hearts, and that the experience of isolation is itself a result of our perceptual abilities not being used to their full capacity.

Single Delight helps to clear our inner vision so that we may see and feel the network of light that energetically connects us with all other living beings. It shows us that this light is always available, always shining, even into what we may consider to be the most shadowy realms of our existence. Its vibration opens our hearts and brings a remembrance of the support we have always had, helping us replace our feelings of isolation with a factual energetic experience of connectedness with life.

The essence of Single Delight is particularly useful for those who are on a path of service that requires them to travel a lot or frequently move to a new location. This activity often brings up painful emotions associated with leaving friends and loved ones behind. Single Delight brings balance to this situation by opening one's awareness of the reality of connectedness without form; connection unlimited by time and space. With this awareness the pain of separation can be felt within the stability of a network of light that exists and is maintained by one's soul family, wherever they might be.

I choose to life this life without strife.
I open my awareness to the source of my difficulties; I am free.

SITKA BURNET *Sanguisorba stipulata*

Sitka Burnet is a perennial belonging to the Rose family. It has a flowering stem that can grow from one to two feet tall. The buds at the lower end of the slim flower-spikes open first, and then progress ringlike up the spike. These white to greenish flowers are sometimes purplish-tinged and are very fragrant. Sitka Burnet can be found blooming in the swamps, bogs, and moist meadows of central Alaska in July and early August.

Indications—feelings of internal discord from unknown origins; feeling bound and limited by one's past; unable to locate the source of one's difficulties in life; having to repeat learning experiences several times before understanding the lessons behind them.

Healing Qualities—The essence of Sitka Burnet addresses a type of internal conflict that is felt as a constant pulling from within; an internal discord from beyond the conscious mind and remembered experience. This essence plunges down into the depths, into the very core of such strife, and illuminates the issues responsible. It then works to bring the different strands of each issue up into the light to be healed and released.

Sitka Burnet works to activate the full potential for healing that lies within a given life lesson. When this essence is indicated in a consultation, it reveals that the individual is prepared to consider all the necessary aspects of a lesson from its beginning point, in this or another lifetime, right up to the present. The gift of this essence is that it helps us to see and understand all the information relevant to a particular lesson so that we can bring that learning experience to completion and release all the energies associated with it.

The Sitka Burnet essence is especially helpful when we encounter deep levels of fear during our inner explorations. It teaches us that we are reacting, not so much to the issues involved or the details of the learning situation, but to all the energy that has been built up around it. Once we have this awareness we can move past this energy and bring the whole dynamic to its healing conclusion.

As I forgive the past, I am empowered in the present.
I exercise my power with love, wisdom, and respect for all beings.

SITKA SPRUCE POLLEN *Picea sitchensis*

Sitka Spruce is the largest tree in Alaska, growing to 160 feet in height and three to five feet in trunk diameter. From the buttressed base, the tall, straight, tapering trunk rises to an open, broad, conical crown with horizontal branches.

The native peoples of southeast Alaska have long considered this spruce to be the most important tree in the forest, possessed of a potent and benevolent spirit. It was also the most useful. The inner bark provided food, sap yielded healing balms, lumber built boats, and roots were woven into baskets.

Sitka Spruce extends from sea level up to about 3,000 feet in the coastal mountains of southeast and southern Alaska, but grows mainly at elevations below 1500 feet.

Indications—power struggles between men and women; reluctance to express or exercise one's power for fear of hurting someone; inequality in relationships with others; lack of humility in one's relationship to the Earth; imbalance between the masculine and feminine expressions of power within an individual.

Healing Qualities—This powerful pollen essence, which could be termed a "grandfather" essence, is a catalyst that supports right action in the present moment through a correct relationship with one's personal power.

Sitka Spruce Pollen is helpful for those who are reluctant to open up and let their power be present. It is for those who fear that their power will in some way harm others if they allow it to come forth into full expression.

This essence facilitates the blending of power and gentleness in an individual, whether they are male or female. As a tree, Sitka Spruce has a strong male presence, and this essence, which is made from pollen grains generated by the male reproductive structure of the tree, carries a very potent quality of yang energy. At the same time, Sitka Spruce emanates a very comforting and consoling vibration–the energetic projection of a great being who is extremely wise and powerful, and very comfortable with that wisdom and power.

Sitka Spruce Pollen clears and expands our energy channels so that we can accept a stronger flow of energy within our body. It encourages us to balance our personal ego so that we can surrender more fully to the truth of our destiny. But most importantly, Sitka Spruce Pollen helps us embody ancient archetypes of mastery in which the masculine and feminine aspects of power are perfectly joined together.

I live in balance with the power of nature.
I relate to nature with fearlessness and love.

SOAPBERRY *Sheperdia canadensis*

Soapberry is a deciduous shrub which grows in dry rocky areas throughout eastern, interior, and southcentral Alaska. This plant is distinct because it often begins to bloom in early May, while there is still snow remaining on the ground. The Soapberry flowers are very tiny, with the male and female blossoms borne on separate bushes.

The female flowers produce small, red, translucent berries which are edible, although their taste is quite bitter. The plant derives its name from the fact that these berries contain saponin, a sugar derivative that causes them to form a lather when beaten.

Indications—muscular tension in the chest, especially around the heart; fear of the power of nature; fear of going out into nature, especially in children; fear of animals; fear of using one's power in irresponsible or inappropriate ways; seeking to have power or domination over others and over nature; unable to keep one's heart open when involved in extremely challenging situations.

Healing Qualities—The essence of Soapberry addresses the issue of our individual acceptance and right use of personal power. Its purpose is to help us learn to balance and harmonize our power with the power of nature.

A significant part of this harmonization process can be achieved through the release of tension that we are holding in and around our hearts, tension created by our fears of the power of nature. The Soapberry essence works on both the perceptual and physical levels to expand our awareness of the fears and emotions that are connected to this tension. It then helps us access the vibrational support from nature herself that we need in order to release these energies from our hearts and physical bodies. Through this grounding and releasing process, we are able to create more space in our lives for the acceptance of our own power and its balanced expression in our environment.

The link between the power of nature and the right use of an individual's personal power is very pertinent at this time in history. There are many cataclysmic events taking place in different regions of the planet. These are, in part, a reflection of the personal power of humans that has gone out of control through not being recognized, accepted, and put to appropriate use.

The essence of Soapberry is offered as a positive catalyst to help bring our collective power as humans back into balance with the power of the Earth, so that we may continue to co-create together for the benefit of all.

My heart contains no judgment; I see clearly.
I surround all inner conflict with acceptance and love.

SPHAGNUM MOSS *Sphagnum sp.*

Sphagnum Moss is an ancient and widespread plant that is common in peat bogs and wet acid areas throughout Alaska.

The color of Sphagnum Moss, which ranges from pale green to vibrant red, is determined by moisture content, so it will change as the relative humidity in the area changes.

Indications—feelings of failure, of never getting it right; overly critical and judgmental of one's healing journey; obsessing about the day-to-day details of one's healing process; unable to see the positive side of transformational experiences.

Healing Qualities—This essence supports our ability to turn inappropriate judgment and criticism into unconditional love and acceptance.

It is not a simple matter to consistently make clear judgments as to whether life is proceeding according to plan. There are times on each individual's path when chaos, confusion, and even disease are essential parts of the journey. When our emotions reach a crisis level, perhaps there is an old pattern that needs to be released. When a person is involved in an accident, it could be a form of experience that the higher self has chosen to initiate a necessary healing process. In each of these instances, the challenge is to be able to clearly perceive, accept, and support the positive change or transformation that is occurring.

This is where our ability to see clearly is so important, and where judgment is most often given in the form of inappropriate criticism, either of ourselves or others. Through a lack of understanding, we will often misinterpret a positive transformational experience as a sign of failure. This habit can leave us filled with a sense of never being able to get it right.

If we truly wish to support the day-to-day evolution of our healing processes, we must learn to recognize our tendencies towards inappropriate criticism before they manifest. Sphagnum Moss helps us learn to open our hearts in that moment when the urge to judge or criticize first appears, and instead clothe the object of our judgment with unconditional love.

This essence encourages us to release the need to criticize or pass harsh judgment on the day-to-day details of our life lessons. It helps us create a place within our hearts that is filled with love and acceptance, so that whenever a core issue or pattern is activated, it will be seen for what it truly is and given all the support it deserves.

I constantly receive nurturing from all living beings.
I accept all support that is offered to me with
openness and gratitude.

SPIRAEA *Spiraea beauverdiana*

Spiraea is a small, widely branching deciduous shrub one to two feet high. Half-rounded clusters of small, fragrant flowers occur at the tips of slender twigs. The flowers are numerous with five white petals that are rose tinged in the center and pink in bud.

Spiraea flowers in late June and early July and its fruits mature in late July and early August. It is common in tundra, swamps, black spruce bogs, muskegs, and forests from lowland to alpine throughout Alaska except Southeast and the North Slope.

Indications—not feeling supported by life; placing conditions and limitations on how support will be allowed into one's life; resistance to growth and expansion; stubbornness; attachment to the way things are, even if they are not to one's liking; unable to recognize the positive while emphasizing the negative.

Healing Qualities—The healing energy of Spiraea is that of a peaceful forest, the beauty of flowers, and the strength of mountains. Its essence helps us open to an awareness of nurturing—the process whereby all living things nourish one another through continual stages of growth.

The Spiraea essence works with our patterns of resistance to growth, our attempts to exist in a static condition independent of the continually evolving forces of change that permeate the living world. It helps us experience life as a flow of energy that is in a constant state of metamorphosis between one form and another.

Spiraea addresses a state of resistance that comes from not feeling supported, a state created by our attachment to the form our support must take in order for us to accept it. When we are in this place of resistance, we can't access the support and nurturing that is available to us.

Spiraea asks us to be unconditional about how support manifests in our lives. It asks us to allow ourselves to receive support for growth and expansion without placing any limitations on how that support is given, and to work with whatever is provided in a spirit of openness and gratitude.

I vigorously release my Divine potential into action.
I move towards my goals with clarity, focus,
and a sense of order.

STICKY GERANIUM *Geranium erianthum*

This variety of geranium is a common field wildflower characterized by five light purple colored petals and palmate leaves.

Sticky Geranium, or cranesbill as it is often called, isn't a plant that waits patiently for its seeds to fall–it is a plant of action. Its seedpods split, curl, and catapult their seeds into the surrounding area.

Indications—tendency to procrastinate; feeling unfocused, lethargic and indecisive; resistance to moving on to the next level or stage of an experience; lacking the energy to reach one's goals; attached to one's current level of consciousness and self-definition.

Healing Qualities—Sticky Geranium is an ideal essence when one feels caught in a web of procrastination. Its vibrant and catalytic energy can help us move from a place of lethargy to a place of decisive and focused action.

This essence stimulates a very focused degree of interaction between the physical, emotional, mental, and spiritual levels of our being. It enables us to move more easily and decisively on to the next level of an experience, whether it be writing the next chapter in a book or making a stronger commitment to a job or relationship, with clarity, focus, and a sense of order.

Sticky Geranium encourages us to tune into our inner knowing and release old levels of programming and resistance that hold us in a place of stagnation. It empowers us to free up our inner potentials and go beyond previous stages of growth and self-definition; to jump into life with energy and enthusiasm.

The essence of Sticky Geranium can be used whenever a person needs additional energy and focus to complete a demanding task, and it has proven especially useful during childbirth, when the mother needs additional support to move on to the next stage of delivering her baby.

I am a radiant being of light.
I empower others to contact their inner authority.

SUNFLOWER *Helianthus annuala*

Sunflowers provide beauty, color, and majesty to the garden. In Alaska, they can grow to a height of 10 to 12 feet when the weather and nutrients are just right.

Every characteristic of this plant exhibits boldness and physical strength. The stalk is as sturdy as a tree trunk, supporting massive heart shaped leaves and an inflorescence of small, yellow, disk and ray florets which together form the familiar Sunflower head.

These hardy flowers help establish and expand energy pathways in the soil and can be planted strategically to increase the penetration of solar energy into certain areas of the garden.

Indications—unbalanced expression of masculine energy, in men or women; weak or dysfunctional relationship to the father, or to one's own identity as a father; resistance to accepting the authority of the higher self; weak sense of being in the world.

Healing Qualities—The essence of Sunflower strengthens the quality of individuality and brings balance to the process of soul activation on the physical plane.

Sunflower helps one attract and activate one's unique spiritual potential in a centered way through the establishment of a grounded, nurturing connection to the Earth. This connection is vital, because without it, an individual's body cannot receive the physical support it needs to allow the spiritual forces to develop to their full potential.

The Sunflower essence also encourages a balanced expression of the masculine or yang quality of universal energy in both men and women. It specifically addresses the creation of a functional relationship with authority, helping us learn how to accept the authority of the higher self, rather than the imposed will of another person.

While Sunflower offers an important essence for both sexes, it is especially helpful for men who need to heal authority issues with their fathers, or pertaining to their own role as a father. For the son, this essence supports the process of solidifying one's personal identity and sense of empowerment. For the father, it imparts a clearer understanding of how to appropriately express authority when needed, and at the same time, support the emerging indentities of one's children.

I live in my own emotional space.
I communicate my emotions with clarity and strength.

SWEETGALE *Myrica gale*

Sweetgale is a medium-sized deciduous shrub growing one to four feet tall. The leaves are about an inch long, and dotted with yellow waxy glands. Twigs are slender, dark brown, with numerous yellow resin dots. This plant is an early bloomer, flowering from mid-May to early June, depending on its location.

Flowers are borne inconspicuously as catkins, with male and female catkins occurring on separate shrubs before the leaves emerge. One of the most unique signatures of Sweetgale is its ability to produce different sexes of flowers on the same shrub in successive years. In other words, a shrub that bears female flowers this season can bear male flowers the next.

Sweetgale is a common shrub of low wet areas, especially bogs. It is a very aromatic plant whose buds, flowers, and leaves can be dried and ground into a powder to be used as a spice, similar in scent to bay leaves.

Indications—inappropriate emotional attachment to others; emotional energies blocked in the lower chakras; emotional communication with others is defensive, lacking clarity, and characterized by conflict, guilt, and the assignment of blame.

Healing Qualities—The Sweetgale flower essence strengthens our ability to relate to others on a feeling level. This plant manifests its healing energies in the unique relationship that exists between the male and female flowers or catkins. These flowers occur on different plants and communicate with each other across the distance that separates them by way of an intense vibrational link.

Sweetgale's stimulating and vibrant energy penetrates deep into our emotional energy centers helping us to identify the old layers of pain and negativity that are affecting the quality of our emotional interactions with others. Once these feelings are recognized, we are better able to understand and complete the lessons connected with them, and allow the corresponding energy blockages to be released.

This essence is very helpful when we are desiring to improve the quality of our emotional interactions in male/female relationships. Sweetgale helps us reclaim our emotional space after an argument or upset, and restores calm and strength to our emotional centers. From this place of balance we are able to respond more directly and appropriately to each other, regardless of the situation.

I consciously bring my healing experiences to completion
on all levels.
I release what is finished.

SWEETGRASS *Hierochloe odorata*

Sweetgrass is an erect, slender and sweet-smelling plant. This perennial, which is also known as Holy Grass or Vanilla Grass, grows throughout Alaska in spruce forests and near river banks.

Its Latin name is derived from the Greek 'hieros' meaning sacred and 'cloe' or grass. American Indians have long used this special grass for ceremonial purposes.

Indications—energy blockages in the etheric body; low energy flow during the day; lack of clarity about how to bring a healing process to final completion; needing to remove disharmonious energies from one's home or work environment.

Healing Qualities—This sacred plant embodies a special quality of energy which can be enjoyed simply by having a certain amount of the dried and bundled grass in one's presence.

As a flower essence, Sweetgrass can lend valuable vibrational support to any healing process and is an important aid in maintaining required levels of clarity and energy.

By opening to the vibration of Sweetgrass on a regular basis, it is possible to cleanse and uplift the physical and etheric bodies so that inharmonious energies do not have a chance to become part of the physical structure. Conversely, the Sweetgrass essence can be taken at the end of a healing process to help release any vibrational debris left over after the cycle has come to completion on the physical level. You may also want to put Sweetgrass in the bath after receiving a massage or any kind of deep body work, to help complete that experience on all levels.

Another effective way to work with this essence is to visualize yourself breathing it into your physical body, and then into your energy field or aura. See the Sweetgrass vibration entering all levels of your being, and with your consciousness guide it to those areas that are most in need of its special properties.

Sweetgrass is also excellent for Space Clearing. Drops of the essence can be added to bowls of water that are placed in selected areas of one's home and work environment, or combined with other purifying essences and essential oils in a misting bottle.

I know who I am and what I can do.
I approach life with confidence and self-determination.

TAMARACK *Larix laricina*

Tamarack is a small to medium sized tree growing from 30 to 60 feet high. It has a tapering trunk four to ten inches in diameter, and horizontal branches extending nearly to the ground. This beautiful tree, sometimes known as larch, is one of the very few deciduous conifers in the world. Its needles turn a beautiful golden color before falling in the autumn. This is a very innovative way to deal with winter because without needles the tree doesn't transpire away precious moisture in desiccating winds and cold. Bare branches also accumulate less snow, so the tree is better able to avoid storm damage.

Tamarack's flowers, male and female, occur on the same branches. The male cones are reddish and covered with scales. The small, dark brown female cones grow singly, open in early autumn and remain attached to the tree in the winter.

Tamarack grows along the edges of bogs, muskegs and other moist locations in open stands with birch, alder, and willow. Its range is from the Brooks Range south to the Alaska Range. It is also widespread throughout most of North America.

Indications—lacking awareness of one's true capacities; weak sense of self-identity; no confidence in one's unique skills and potentials; identifying with the outer manifestation of problems and difficulties rather than with one's ability to resolve them.

Healing Qualities—The unique growth characteristics of Tamarack mark it an individual among the needle-bearing trees of the Earth.

The essence of Tamarack helps us maintain a conscious, grounded connection with the source of our own individuality. Its vibration enhances our awareness of who we are and strengthens the knowing of our true selves, our unique abilities, and what we can do.

When we are faced with a challenge, such as moving to a new area and taking on a new job, there can be a tendency to place a great deal of our attention, and thus our identity, on the situation and the conditions connected with it.

Tamarack helps us use this opportunity to identify instead with the essence of who we are, so that we remain confident and centered in the knowledge that our abilities will carry us through.

I allow the power of Spirit to be communicated through
me in every moment.
My highest motivation is my love for life.

TUNDRA ROSE *Potentilla fruticosa*

Tundra Rose is a many branched deciduous shrub growing from one to five feet high. Leaves are alternate and occur on slender, light brown twigs.

Individual flowers occur at the base of the leaves or in terminal clusters. They are composed of a saucer-shaped base with five rounded spreading yellow petals.

Tundra Rose flowers from June to August and its fruits mature from July to September. It is common in the moist soils of swamps, on the borders of streams and lakes, and on dry, rocky hillsides throughout most of mainland Alaska.

Indications—motivated by fears, especially the fear of dying; fulfills life's daily tasks without joy or pleasure; uninspired; communication with one's higher self is difficult or lacks clarity; unable to express abstract concepts and ideas in clear and concise terms.

Healing Qualities—This essence is for those who have much to offer, but who have lost hope and are close to giving up on what they came to this Earth to do. Through its bright yellow flowers, Tundra Rose communicates a love for life that resonates deep within the heart. Its vibration is an affirmation of the power of life over death, and of the potential of form completely infused with spirit.

The essence of Tundra Rose gently brings our deepest fears of living into the light of love, so that we may be motivated by a love of life rather than a fear of death. Our alignment with this higher level of motivation strengthens our ability to complete the challenging tasks we have chosen to undertake in our daily lives, and helps us bring a larger expression of joy into the process of their fulfillment.

Tundra Rose is also an important essence for those who have chosen a path of service and healing through communication. It catalyzes a stronger connection between the spiritual realms and our conscious selves, helping our words become living expressions of higher knowledge and spiritual truth.

I open fully to the healing power of love.
I release all density into light.

TUNDRA TWAYBLADE *Listera cordata*

Tundra Twayblade grows in mossy forest and meadow habitats in the southern and central parts of Alaska. Its tiny flowers and twin heart shaped leaves are supported by a single stem which can grow up to 12 inches tall.

Indications—blocking the healing power of love from reaching those areas of the body that are most in need of it; shock and trauma in humans and animals; deep pain and anguish, often resulting from past experiences of abuse; unable to feel love in the heart.

Healing Qualities—Abuse is one of the most prevalent dysfunctional patterns on the Earth. It is an issue of great importance to any individual who has experienced it and to the human race as a whole. The positive news is that the many manifestations of abuse which have occurred throughout human history are currently being acknowledged on deeper levels than ever before.

Working with a powerful karmic theme such as abuse, however, can be a very intense experience. The process can be accompanied by surprisingly deep levels of pain and anguish, especially when an individual is not aware of the fact that when they contact their own experiences they will also be touching into the larger archetype of abuse as it exists on the planet.

Tundra Twayblade emphasizes the importance of working through the heart when we are called to heal such deeply held issues and traumas. Its primary action is to strengthen the power of the heart so it may serve as the central fulcrum, or balance point, for the entire healing process.

This essence specifically addresses the human tendency to compartmentalize the pain and suffering that can result from an experience of abuse. The problem with this response is, in our efforts to insulate ourselves from the strong feelings we have about these experiences, we also block healing energy from being able to reach those places that are most in need of it.

Tundra Twayblade helps us reverse this situation by opening our hearts to a laser like quality of Unconditional Love. This finely focused energy catalyzes the release of constrictions in the heart that deny the healing power of love access to those areas where the cellular memory of the abuse is still present. As we accept this love into our cells, an alchemical transformation occurs, and we are forever free from the abusive experience. In this way, Tundra Twayblade empowers us to completely release the impact of abuse from our lives, and in doing so, to weaken the entire pattern of abuse on the planet.

I listen with inner presence, calm and neutrality.
I communicate with intention and clarity.

TWINFLOWER *Linnaea borealis*

Twinflower is a creeping evergreen dwarf shrub with long, slender, above ground runners that branch and take root in the leaf litter. The small, pink, trumpet shaped flowers are usually paired and face opposite directions.

Twinflower is a common ground cover in the open forests of Alaska and is circumpolar in range.

Indications—defensive and reactive communication; having a lot to say, but no way to say it; difficulty listening to and understanding what others are trying to communicate; unable to communicate clearly with different aspects of the self; already having opinions formed before hearing what another has to say.

Healing Qualities—Twinflower is an essence for anyone who would like to improve their skills as a listener, speaker, or both. It addresses two of the most important requirements of good communication: presence and neutrality.

In a conversation, we must first be present for the other person before we can truly hear what they are saying. When we are agitated or distracted, we are not available to receive their words or understand the information contained within them. Then there are instances when we have difficulty not reacting to what a person is saying, especially when their words are delivered in a way that is meant to elicit an emotional response from us.

This tiny, delicate flower projects a very focused quality of calm energy that can help us identify and let go of the distractions that keep us from being present during a conversation. It also supports the creation of heart centered objectivity, a quality that enables us to maintain our neutrality even when we receive an emotionally charged communication from another person.

This inner presence, calm, and neutrality can also serve us when we wish to speak and be heard by others. In this context, the Twinflower essence can help us create our words with a focused intent, and project them with a clarity of energy that will help others hear and understand the essence of what we have to say.

As a plant, Twinflower expresses poise, balance, and beauty with a gentle and refined energy. As an essence, she reminds us that when we express our words from a place of calm clarity and inner strength, and offer our full presence and attention to all who speak to us, we elevate the art of communication.

I exchange my pain from the past for the pleasure of life
in the present.
Each trauma I heal is a gift to all.

WHITE FIREWEED *Epilobium angustifolium*

Fireweed is a nutritious, wild edible plant that has a reputation as an astringent and anti-inflammatory herb. This species of fireweed ranges over extensive areas of Alaska along roads and in meadows, forests, and especially recently burned areas. The occurrence of white flowered fireweed is extremely rare and unpredictable.

Indications—deep emotional shock and trauma in humans and animals; profound alienation from the body after an experience of sexual or emotional abuse; over-identification with a traumatic experience; tendency to repeatedly injure the same part of the body; difficulty letting go of physical and emotional pain.

Healing Qualities—This essence was collected from fireweed plants with white blossoms. These plants were growing in a small area surrounded by an acre or so of fireweed with magenta blooms. Botanically speaking, this display of different colored flowers on plants of the same species is called an anomaly. Energetically speaking, the occurrence of White Fireweed is a response within the plant kingdom to a need on the planet for profound emotional healing.

The essence of White Fireweed is very calming to the emotional body after it has suffered a recent emotional shock or trauma. This essence also supports the complete healing of any painful experiences from the past by helping us remove the energetic imprint of those experiences from our cellular memory. This is very important, because as long as this memory is present in some part of the body, there will be a degree of personal identification with it, and this will support the tendency to attract similar experiences in the future.

White Fireweed encourages us to surrender our emotional pain and trauma by offering to exchange it for a very pure matrix of healing energy. The body consciousness recognizes that with the support of this energy it can let go, and as it does, this healing matrix moves into the area that was holding the trauma. Its presence then enables that area to begin a process of regeneration and renewal that will subsequently be supported by the body's own healing powers.

All aspects of my being are unified in present action.
I live in balance between Earth and sky.

WHITE SPRUCE *Picea glauca*

White Spruce is the largest and most common tree of interior Alaska. This conifer intermingles with birch and aspen on well drained soils with southern exposure and on sandy soils along the edges of lakes and rivers, where running water thaws the soil. It is seldom found where permafrost is close to the surface.

White Spruce grows from 40 to 70 feet high and six to 18 inches in diameter. It has a pointed crown and slightly drooping branches with upturned ends and many small drooping side twigs.

Indications—feeling disintegrated; polarized into inaction; soul forces have split off from the physical body; connected to higher knowledge, but unable to apply it to life's challenges in a practical way; unable to integrate feelings with the logical dictates of the mind.

Healing Qualities—Of the many plants growing in the interior of the state, Native Alaskans consider Spruce to be the most important. Besides being a major source of spiritual nourishment in Native legends, White Spruce continues to fill the physical needs of food, shelter, and medicine.

White Spruce is the gentle grandfather healer. It is deeply rooted to the Earth, yet it is in constant communication with the cosmos. It offers us a touchstone to our own higher knowledge. If we open to it in an attunement, it will illuminate those aspects of our wisdom that are useful, and show us how we can best bring them into our current situation.

The essence of White Spruce helps us live our day-to-day lives with balance and stability. It helps us transcend our inner polarities to bring logic, intuition, spirit, and emotion together into unified action in the present moment.

This essence is especially helpful when there has been a disconnection or a "splitting off" of the soul forces from the physical body. This level of inner separation can be found in people who have encountered an extreme level of trauma in their lives, and have decided that in order to survive they must pull their soul energy away from the circuitry of the physical self, which is attempting to hold all the pain from these experiences.

With the help of the White Spruce essence, these individuals are able to reconnect with all levels of the self and begin the process of retrieving and reintegrating these fragments of soul energy within the physical body, leading them to an experience of true wholeness once again.

I trust my higher self.
My sensitivities are fully present with me here and now.

WHITE VIOLET *Viola renifolia*

White Violets grow on south facing slopes in the birch forests of the interior of Alaska. These small delightful white and purple veined flowers are some of the earliest blooming plants, often appearing in mid-May. They rise up through the leaf litter on the forest floor to bloom while their heart shaped leaves are still unfolding.

Indications—hypersensitive; uncomfortable in closed-in spaces and constrained environments; hesitant to initiate contact with others; distrustful; insecure when out in public; fearful of losing one's identity in a group; unable to embody one's sensitivity in a comfortable way.

Healing Qualities—The delicate White Violet blossoms offer an essence of purity–an essence of vibrational support for those who have a very sensitive and pure nature.

Highly sensitive people have unique requirements when it comes to setting and maintaining functional energy boundaries. Such people are acutely aware of their surroundings, and if their boundaries are not appropriate and intact, they will often feel that their personal space is being infringed upon, and will be reluctant to allow themselves to be fully present.

This feeling can become very pronounced, and at times almost intolerable, when sensitive individuals find themselves in constrained environments, such as on a crowded plane during a long overseas flight, where the actual physical space allotted to each person is very limited.

The White Violet essence supports the creation of new energy boundaries by helping us open a conscious, two-way flow of communication between the physical body and the higher self. This connection encourages the energy of Divine trust to build and strengthen in the aura in response to our specific need for safety and security, and to become incorporated into the energetic structure of the new boundary as it is created.

As this quality of trust becomes anchored into the energy field, we can begin to relax and allow more of our personal energy and sensitivity to be present regardless of the dynamics of our environment.

I appreciate and freely share my inner beauty with others.
I relax into my Divine creative potential.

WILD IRIS *Iris setosa*

Wild Iris generally occurs in meadows and along shores of lakes and ponds throughout the southern two-thirds of Alaska. It is a strikingly beautiful plant that employs several creative methods to insure its survival.

Wild Iris grows from short, thick, branching rootstalks which have the ability to store water and release it to the plant as needed. The flowers are conspicuous because of the three erect petals, the three reflexed sepals, and the three petal-like branches of the style which serve to direct rain and the sun's energy to the center of the flower.

The blooming cycle of this plant is very rapid, often taking only two days to move from the bud stage to maturity.

Indications—lack of trust in one's own capacity to create; blocking one's creative expression because of an unwillingness to share oneself with others; unfocused creativity; not feeling connected to universal sources of inspiration.

Healing Qualities—Wild Iris addresses several states of mind that can affect our ability to create. One is a lack of awareness that we have an unlimited amount of creative energy available to us and that it comes from a Divine source. Another is an absence of appreciation-of ourselves, of the beauty around us, and of our contributions to the world. A third is an unwillingness to share ourselves and our creativity with others. Any one of these mental attitudes can create an inner tension or lead to an excess of effort that will hinder or stop our creative flow altogether.

The Wild Iris essence helps us create new thought structures that encourage the free flowing expression of our creative energies. It helps us recognize the beautiful expression of Divine creativity that we are, and supports our willingness to share our beauty and creative presence freely with others. This in turn stimulates our awareness of the creative potential we hold within and encourages us to allow this creativity to flow forth in a relaxed and focused way from the center of our beings.

When guidance speaks, my heart opens and my mind receives.
My mind is a miracle of flexibility.

WILD RHUBARB *Polygonum alaskanum*

Wild Rhubarb is a stately plant, often growing to six feet in height. It occurs in large showy clumps on roadsides and in open woods and river margins throughout most of Alaska.

This perennial has a thick root and a somewhat woody, branched stem. Its leaves are smooth, medium green above and lighter green beneath. The widely branching inflorescence is a mass of tiny flowers which bloom from late June to early August.

Indications—mental inflexibility; uninspired; unreceptive; stagnant perspective on life; mental rigidity blocking the heart from opening to Divine guidance; mind controlled by fear-based impulses; mind and heart working at cross-purposes with each other.

Healing Qualities—The essence of Wild Rhubarb promotes mental flexibility and creative problem solving by clearing and expanding the channel of communication between the higher self, the heart, and the mind.

This essence helps the mind move into and occupy its true position, that of being under the control and guidance of the higher self and Divine Will. The mind is designed to be of service to us, but we often allow it to occupy a position that is subordinate to the ego. When we let the mind control us from this place, the result can be a life that runs along chaotic lines far removed from higher purpose.

Wild Rhubarb works to reverse this situation by helping us bring the mind back into alignment with the higher self. It does this in two ways. The first is by cleansing the channel between the mind and the heart; dislodging blockages or barriers to the flow of energy between these two centers. As this flow begins to move more strongly, the process of surrendering the mind to the heart can begin, or move to a deeper level—whatever is possible at the time.

The second is by helping us open our hearts to the impulses of the higher self. When this flow is strengthened and the channel between the heart and mind is clear, the higher self has constant access to the mind, and a relaxation of inappropriate mental control will follow. New thoughts, new perspectives, new plans for action, and new solutions to problems will be the result.

I create positive reality from the quality of my thoughts.
I take responsibility for what I have created.

WILLOW *Salix bebbiana*

This willow is typically referred to as Bebb or Diamond Willow. It is distinguishable by its one or more trunks of up to nine inches in diameter and its generally shrubby habit. The common name refers to the diamond shaped depressions at the junctions where the trunk branches.

The male and female catkins first emerge in the spring as pussy willows, elongating for fertilization as spring progresses. The catkins are small, green, hairy spikelets of unisexual flowers, borne on short, leafy stalks. Bebb Willow is widely distributed throughout Alaska's interior and south to the gulf coast.

Willow is an excellent source of vitamin C, and also contains significant amounts of salicin, a natural form of aspirin that was traditionally used as an anti-inflammatory. Native Alaskans twisted willow bark into twine for nets and fishing line, and the supple twigs are still used for weaving baskets and stretching hides. Eskimos also chew the fresh willow and apply the paste to insect stings to relieve the pain and swelling.

Indications—inflexibility; refusing to take responsibility for one's actions or for the life one has created; blaming others for one's problems and difficulties; resistance to hearing new ideas or new ways of doing things.

Healing Qualities—The energy of Willow is receptivity and resilience. It grows surrounded by water, which it takes up and transforms into new growth. It is flexible, bending gracefully before the wind and yielding under heavy snows. Willow also displays an amazing degree of tenacity by growing new branches each spring after being nibbled on by moose during the winter.

The family signature of Willow is very strong, with all plants receiving physical and vibrational support from each other. The Willow essence echoes this quality by promoting the unification of ideas within a group of people, especially ideas originating from their collective higher consciousness.

But most importantly, the Willow flower essence helps us remove our resistance to consciously creating our lives. It helps us become aware of and then dissolve self-imposed mental limitations, so that we may come into a greater alignment with universal principles of thought and illumination.

This essence helps us give birth to positive life experiences by asking us to take a greater level of conscious responsibility for our own creative mental processes. As we embody the attitudes of flexible mind and resilient under-standing, we are at peace and find joy in the act of living.

I am the source of my own protection.
I attract only those energies that are in harmony with
my highest good.

YARROW *Achillea borealis*

Yarrow grows 12 to 24 inches high from a slender, freely branching rhizome, or underground stem. The plant is topped by a flat cluster of small white or faintly pink aromatic flowers, blooming until late summer. The leaves have a ferny appearance; a closely related species name, millefolium, is literally translated to mean "a thousand leaves".

Yarrow ranges throughout the state in meadows, sandy slopes, and along roadsides.

Indications—oversensitive to the environment; tendency to absorb the energy of others; distracted by outside influences; looking for protection from outside rather than from within the self; integrity of the aura has been compromised by injury and trauma in this or another lifetime.

Healing Qualities—The best known historical medicinal use of Yarrow was to staunch the flow of blood. The genus name, Achillea, is from the Greek god-hero Achilles who reportedly carried the plant with him to treat wounded soldiers. In the garden, Yarrow gives strength to neighboring plants, making them more disease resistant.

The Yarrow plant gives off a strong aura of protective energy. As this energy radiates from its source it automatically carries off any lower or inharmonious energies. Therefore, the Yarrow plant does not attract any negative influences but rather enhances the energy of its surroundings.

Yarrow's powerful vibration helps us expand our awareness of the integrity of our energy field by reflecting its qualities back to us. Guided by this reflection, we are given the opportunity to strengthen those areas that are weak and reactive to outside influences. As we work with this process, we come to the realization that our only true protection is the clarity and power of the light that radiates from within our being.

This essence is also applicable wherever there is a need to strengthen the aura against known environmental hazards, such as the electromagnetic radiation from computers and florescent lights, and from the electronics on modern aircraft.

I understand the continuum of my life experience.
I look for the edge of the known and step beyond.

YELLOW DRYAS *Dryas drummondii*

Yellow Dryas is a dwarf evergreen shrub that grows in extensive, dense mats on gravel bars, lake shores and scree slopes. The leaves are leathery, with deeply notched margins, and are a distinctive dark green above and silvery-white below. Flowers occur individually at the top of sturdy stems, their yellow petals never opening fully.

Yellow Dryas flowers from mid-June through July with its fruits maturing in late July and August. It is a pioneering plant and is often found on gravel bars of flood plains.

Indications—feeling unsupported and isolated; disconnected or estranged from one's soul family; unsure of one's connection to the larger picture; unable to sense the connective thread that links one's experiences into a coherent and understandable whole.

Healing Qualities—The healing quality of Yellow Dryas may be seen in its pioneering growth pattern. A new plant gets its start from a fertile seed and sends roots into the soil, which is generally devoid of other plant growth. This primary plant then extends runners outward on top of the ground, and flowers occur near the outermost tip of each runner. After the flower petals have wilted, the styles elongate in a clockwise swirling pattern and expand into a fully opening seed head which releases copious amounts of feathery seed plumes.

This pattern is repeated yearly by each plant until a dense mat is formed. During the blossoming season a majority of the flowers can be seen forming a ring around the expanding edge of the mat. Eventually, these mats will grow to within several inches of each other, until they have almost completely covered the available ground.

Yellow Dryas offers a very powerful vibration of support for those who are pioneers, a category that includes everyone–we are all covering new ground in our lives, and infusing new areas of our world with light. It helps us maintain a clear perspective on the myriad aspects of our individual and collective cycles of growth and expansion, and retain a grounding to our greater family identity as we move through dynamic cycles of change.

This essence is very helpful whenever we feel isolated or are confused about our identity and purpose within the larger scheme of things. It enables us to draw what we need from the source of all life through the connective thread of our experience.

Part Four

The Alaskan
Environmental Essences

I open my life to receive all manifestations of Divine support.
I draw on the wellsprings of eternal Light,
so that I may become Light.

CHALICE WELL

Background Information—This essence was made in the Chalice Well Gardens of Glastonbury, England, with water from the Chalice Well. The bowl containing this water was placed in several significant locations throughout the garden, in moonlight and sunlight, to allow it to be infused with the angelic, elemental, plant and mineral energies that were present there.

Healing Qualities—Visiting the Chalice Well is an experience of pure grace. The frequency of energy emanating from this sacred well blesses and sustains all equally, without judgement or rancor.

The Chalice Well Gardens are a supreme example of unconditional love and support: the well of flowing water that never stops, the carefully tended flowers and trees–so much love from the Goddess expressed through a myriad of forms.

The Chalice Well environmental essence connects us to the profoundly personal and eternal support that is constantly available from the angelic, elemental, plant, and mineral kingdoms. It's message is that we are not alone. We are a part of the entire web of life and All That Is and we can draw upon this matrix of support whenever we feel lost or need help to take the next step on our life's path.

This essence connects us to forms and levels of support beyond our current awareness. It does this by challenging the belief systems and emotional blockages that we allow to stand in the way of a stronger connection to the Source. What often comes up is a judgment that says we don't deserve the support we need because of our past actions. The Chalice Well essence reminds us that it doesn't matter what our personal history is–the support is still there, just as strong and pure as it always was. Our perceptions may change and the form of our experiences will change, but the grace of unconditional love remains constant.

We have noticed over the years that Chalice Well is one of our essences most often given to children. Their natural state is to live in grace, accepting and loving others. When there are fears of any sort, their hearts often close down in protection. The Chalice Well essence helps children to feel safe and supported by their environment and by the angels, and is a favorite to place in a spray bottle to mist the child's room before bedtime.

I open my life to the Light of Truth; I ask that nothing
shall remain hidden from it.
I take responsibility for my feelings.

FULL MOON REFLECTION

Background Information—This essence was made on a cold clear winter night, in a canyon overlooking Kachemak Bay in southcentral Alaska. A bowl of water was positioned on the snow so that it would receive the direct light of the full moon, and also the moonlight reflecting off the water of the bay and from the white, snow-filled canyon.

Healing Qualities—The full moon is a time of cosmic alignment when the light of the sun is reflected off the fully revealed face of the moon onto the Earth. This light shining in the darkness affects us all, and not always in subtle ways.

The light contained within this essence penetrates deep into our shadow selves to illuminate that which lies unresolved beneath the surface of our consciousness. As we open ourselves to this light, we have the opportunity to let go of many of the subconscious patterns that are affecting us and others in ways beyond our current understanding.

It is a common tendency to project these subconscious patterns onto others rather than claiming them as our own. A typical example is when we feel a certain uncomfortable emotion and then blame another person for making us feel that way. We then expect that individual to change their behavior so we can feel more comfortable. In relationships, this inclination can take on a much higher level of complexity.

Relationships create an ongoing series of opportunities for uncovering old issues and habits of behavior that need to be brought to the surface, acknowledged, and released. We are often unable to see the impact of these patterns on ourselves, but when they are unconsciously projected into the shared dynamic of a relationship, their impact becomes obvious. How we deal with this impact will determine, to a large degree, the health of the relationship. If a closer and more harmonious partnership is to be achieved, we must be willing to shine the light of truth on these projections so that we can take responsibility for them and deal with the issues they represent in an honest manner.

The Full Moon Reflection essence is very supportive of this process but it will be most effective when both people take it at the same time. When used in this context, it can help increase the degree of honesty and disclosure in the relationship by bringing awareness to unresolved issues which are being mutually suppressed and projected, so they can be resolved with reciprocal acceptance, understanding, and compassion.

I willingly release that which is no longer in my highest truth.
I flow with the strong, cleansing current
of ever-changing life.

GLACIER RIVER

Background Information—This essence of solarized glacier water was prepared below the terminus of the Gulkana Glacier in the central Alaska Range.

The water emerging from the base of this glacier carries fine particles of rock–the remains of a mountain eroded over the years by the constant pressure and movement of glacial ice. This silt, or rock flour as it is sometimes called, is so concentrated that it turns the water gray. The area where this water was collected is immensely powerful. In its continuing cycles of advance and retreat, the glacier has carved a wide valley out of the mountain, leaving huge boulders and tall hills of gravel in its wake.

Healing Qualities—The Glacier River essence is for those who are attached to the current form of their lives, even when there is every indication that it needs to change. The weight of our present potential always moves the past into position to be released. This essence teaches us that if we are to truly accept and embody change, we must always be willing to let go of the form of what has been. Only then can we co-create and honor the new form of what is to be.

The message of the Glacier River essence is that change is inevitable and constant. Humans constantly dance around this truth, thinking about change and planning to change, but usually favoring the status quo. With some, it is a matter of resistance. Others feel they just don't have the energy required to make it through the change that is being called for.

Glacier River addresses a type of stubbornness where we think we are stronger than the forces of change. Our attitude is to just stand our ground and not let anything push us around. This tenacity is admirable when it is being used in pursuit of our life purpose. However, if it is being used to maintain a static position, sooner or later the current of change will tip us over.

The power of Glacier River is that it can meet the strongest resistance that we are capable of putting forth, and direct the energy caught up in this resistance towards the realization of our destiny. As we surrender to the elemental power contained within this essence, we cease to worry about what might happen if things were to change. Instead, we trust our inner compass, sit back, and enjoy the scenery as it rushes by.

I transform resistance with focused awareness.
I ennoble change with consciousness.

GREENLAND ICECAP

Background Information—This environmental essence was prepared on the island of Greenland using water taken from an ice-blue glacial lake.

Greenland is the largest island in the world. Eighty-five percent of its surface is covered by a thick cap of ice, the second largest mass of ice in the world. This ice is in constant movement, from its center divide to its outer edges, where large pieces of numerous glaciers continuously break off into the sea. This essence was prepared on a part of the ice cap which overlays an area where two of the Earth's continental plates are slowly pulling away from each other.

Healing Qualities—The Greenland Icecap essence embodies energy created by the natural, subterranean movement of the Earth's crust, cleansed and clarified by its journey upwards through a two thousand-foot layer of ice.

This essence helps us expand our sensitivity to the energetic shifts that are constantly taking place in the Earth. It can also assist us in becoming more aware of our own subterranean impulses for change, and of the subconscious fears that can obstruct these impulses and lead to shock waves of personal upheaval.

Our fears, and the various levels of resistance that result from them, are present in our lives for a reason. They contain essential information and the seed potential of our future selves. Greenland Icecap can help us learn how to embrace, rather than fight against these fears, so they can become an important source of direction and guidance for our movement from the old to the new.

The plates of the Earth's crust give us a profound example of how it is possible to constantly surrender into the inevitability of change, but in a measured and focused way. Earthquakes result when these massive life forms release energy created by the friction between them, but if they had no resistance to each other, there would be no stability on the planet. We want to have some resistance in our lives, but how do we find the balance between holding on and letting go? Greenland Icecap addresses both sides of the issue.

To those who are locked into inaction, this essence brings a greater awareness of the internal dynamics of their resistance and how to work with it. On the opposite side are those who are moving so much with the flow that they no longer have a stable self identity. For these individuals, Greenland Icecap can impart the much needed qualities of strength and solidity, enabling them to slow down and assess what has been going on in their lives. In all instances, this essence can help us learn to channel the energy generated by our fears, impulses, and desires into positive forward movement in our lives.

I bathe my body, mind, and soul in the cleansing
waters of creation.
I surrender that which obscures my God given innocence.

LIARD HOT SPRINGS

Background Information—This essence was co-created at Liard Hot Springs in the extreme northern part of British Columbia, Canada. It was prepared on a crystal clear, -30°F winter day.

Healing Qualities—The water used to prepare this environmental essence was captured as it bubbled forth into the pool, having been propelled on its long journey up through the Earth's crust by intense pressure and heat.

In all natural hot springs we find an outpouring of the forces of creation, a re-creation of the primordial energies of paradise, a powerful reminder of what it was like on Earth before the cumulative actions and energies of human beings began to collect in the planetary aura.

The healing gift that these forces of creation carry is an original archetype of innocence. As we enter and relax into the calming vibrations of this essence, we are cleansed of layer after layer of the energetic grit and grime we have collected during our lifetimes on this planet. This cleansing brings us back in touch with the innocent truth of who we really are–spiritual beings who have come to this Earth to learn.

The Liard Hot Springs essence can help us come to this awareness of innocence regardless of our current levels of self-blame and incrimination. One of the more difficult situations is when there is a sense of guilt that is way out of proportion to the remembered events of one's lifetime. This accumulation of guilt from other lifetimes is one of the main reasons some people are repeat offenders. Such persons have lost their innocence. Their sense of identity and self-worth is contaminated with negative feelings about the mistakes and choices they have made, and this keeps them bound to the old patterns of behavior that continually reinforce this perspective.

The essence of Liard Hot Springs is capable of completely clearing these kinds of ancient patterns from our energy fields, minds, and emotions. It can help us surrender whatever guilt or despair we have about our past actions in a spirit of renewal. Then we can enter into a place where everything is possible, for it is in the light of our original child-like innocence that we can discover and manifest our full potential.

I open my heart to the forces of creation.
I reunite with the true essence of my being.

NORTHERN LIGHTS

Background Information—This environmental essence was prepared on a windy, -30°F arctic night under a magnificent swirling display of green northern lights.

This phenomenon of light, also called the aurora borealis, has its origins on the sun. The sun is continuously sending out a stream of charged particles of energy that travel through space as solar wind. As this solar wind reaches the Earth's magnetic field these particles are drawn toward the north and south geomagnetic poles. When these solar electrons meet the Earth's upper atmosphere they collide with gas molecules, causing those molecules to enter into an excited state called ionization. The light displays we see are produced when these ionized gas molecules return to their normal or "ground" state.

Healing Qualities—These "rainbows of the night" have the power to liberate us from a mundane and earthbound perspective on life through the vehicle of our amazement. As we gaze at their wondrous oscillations of light and energy, we are given the opportunity to expand our senses beyond the physical and join in a dance with the source of our creation.

This essence is often indicated when we are poised on the edge of a breakthrough in consciousness, but lack the energy to complete the process. In this instance, Northern Lights can help us tap into the fundamental creation forces of the Universal Field and gather the energy we need to make the transition from the old to the new.

The essence of Northern Lights has the capacity to work with our energy patterns at an archetypal level. As this essence was prepared under a green aurora, its healing focus is to support deep levels of re-patterning in the heart.

Northern Lights is a particularly useful essence to take after an experience of deep transformation, especially when such an experience has broken down the old energetic patterns of connection that we have used to relate to others and to the outside world. This can leave us feeling disoriented, and with our heart forces scattered. It is in this place of dissolution and disintegration that the essence of Northern Lights does its work, helping us create a new energetic matrix of connection in our hearts based on Universal Love.

My inner space is filled with quiet simplicity.
I have all the time I need.

POLAR ICE

Background Information—*Note: In 1988, a friend named Doug Buchanan had the opportunity to parachute into an area near the North Pole to help set up an aircraft landing strip for a government expedition. While there, Doug was able to collect this environmental essence from the Arctic Ocean ice pack. The following information has been excerpted from his own account of the experience.*

The Polar Ice essence was collected on the Arctic Ocean ice pack near the North Pole, at 88 degrees north latitude, 94 degrees east longitude.

The Arctic Ocean ice pack is a skim of ice, ± 15 feet thick, covering an area over 1,000 miles in diameter. It is a crazed jigsaw of ice floes, pressure ridges of jumbled ice, and windblown snow. This ice is in motion, floating on a deep ocean. Two major currents in the Arctic Ocean keep the ice moving from its freezing origins to its thawing release. In different areas this transition may take from three to ten or more years.

Healing Qualities—The Polar ice pack is an austere environment where little except ice can be noticed with superficial observation. Since the distractions of our common surroundings are absent, one's mind quickly becomes attuned to the richness of subtleties.

This essence addresses our relationship to time and transition. It represents the energy of pure time, of pure waiting, without any goal other than to wait for the transition to complete its cycle. It is about time that rests from reasoning or intent, time carried by forces of pure transition.

The Polar Ice essence can be used to support us when we are impatient with a cycle of change, when we want it to be a different time than it is in our lives. Perhaps we are concerned with getting older, waiting for an operation, or in between relationships or jobs. Most of the time, we really don't know what's going to happen next. Our challenge is to remain present with ourselves and our process and accept where we are in each moment.

The unusual strength and purity of this environmental essence empowers us to stay present in a place that is seemingly suspended in time, a place where we are able to simply wait, with no ties to the past and no anticipation of what is to come. From this clear space we are able to start new cycles of experience that are not influenced by our attachments to the past or our worries about the future.

I surrender all that is no longer useful or
necessary in my life.
My energy field is clean, clear, and vibrantly alive.

PORTAGE GLACIER

Background Information—This glacial essence was collected at Portage Lake in southcentral Alaska. Portage Lake sits at the terminus of the Portage Glacier, which is one of the more accessible glaciers in the vast Chugiak Icefield.

For this essence, a bowl was filled with glacial water and placed near the shore of the lake where it caught the first rays of the morning sun as they began to shine through the fog and mists rising from the surface of the water.

Healing Qualities—All glaciers are massive generators of energy particles called negative ions. Portage Glacier, like most other glaciers in the world, is getting smaller. As it retreats, more and more of these negative ions are released into the atmosphere where they cleanse, renew, and revitalize the air that we breathe. The water used to prepare this essence contains these ionized energy particles as well as a powerful mix of energies created from a dynamic series of elemental interactions.

These interactions start at the glacier itself. Because of the extreme weight of accumulated snow, the ice at the front, or terminus, of the glacier is constantly being pushed forward. This causes large pieces to continually break off, or calve, into the lake. Once in the water, these chunks of ice are blown about by the constant wind coming off the icefield and warmed by the sun on clear days. As they drift across the lake they slowly melt away, all the while releasing energy into the air and water. This process is repeated endlessly throughout the summer months, and it is this dramatic and timeless interplay of the elements that is captured within this essence.

The Portage Glacier environmental essence is an extremely powerful catalyst for cleansing that can be used to clear physical toxins from the body. It can also facilitate the release of outdated thoughts, belief systems, and emotional patterns that are no longer useful, necessary, or contributing to our health and well-being.

This essence is also a particularly powerful tool for purifying toxic or polluted environments. It is able to break up and release patterns of stagnant energy, such as you would find in a room that has been closed up for a long time, or where there has been addiction, depression, or abuse. It then moves this energy completely out of the space being cleansed, replacing it with the pure, elementally infused energy of nature.

I honor the physical world with my grounded presence.
I balance the Earth and cosmos within my physical body.

RAINBOW GLACIER

Background Information—This essence was prepared from water taken at the terminus of Rainbow Glacier, which is located high in the Alaska Range in the eastern part of the state.

The water emerging from the base of this glacier carries not only the physical particles of ground-up rock, but also the vibrational imprint of thousands of years of force, pressure, and the climatic interactions of sun, wind, and extreme cold.

Healing Qualities—The environmental essence prepared from this glacial water provides a grounding and balancing force for those who are having difficulty connecting to the physical plane.

Much of this difficulty comes from the fact that these individuals are very strongly focused in the celestial realms or in the higher dimensions. They do not know how to ground their relationship with cosmic energy into the physical dimension of time and space, where it can be better understood by the mind and integrated by the body.

The Rainbow Glacier essence offers such persons a pure and powerful frequency of Earth elemental energy that they can use as a bridge to find their way here. This essence also functions as a kind of energetic staircase which they can use to descend one step at a time as they get used to denser levels of third dimensional energy.

This essence also works to alleviate deep levels of resistance to being present in one's body, resistance that is often the result of an extremely painful experience. In this instance, a person may have been well grounded before the experience, but has reacted to it by becoming less connected to their body and to the Earth.

In this context the Rainbow Glacier essence would help the individual reestablish their grounding connection, and also help them release the traumatic energy from the experience, so that they can once again feel at home in their body and on the Earth.

I dance in celebration of the elemental powers of the Earth.
I am cleansed by rainbow showers of Light.

SOLSTICE STORM

Background Information—During my summers as a fire fighter in the Alaskan bush, I became very familiar with the massive storm systems that circulated around the state. Part of my job was to monitor weather conditions that would lead to the formation of thunderstorms and to the lightning strikes that would ignite wildfires.

At Lake Minchumina, on summer solstice day in 1984, I had the opportunity to meet one of these storm clouds on a more personal level and co-create an environmental essence with it.

I first became aware of this impressive thundercloud, which spanned a distance of about twenty-five miles from edge to edge, when it was still ten or fifteen miles away. It had a very powerful presence and was advancing slowly but directly toward my position on the northeast shore of the lake.

As the cloud moved closer, its circumference became infused with a pink light, and the fine mist of water droplets emerging from its base became a shimmering veil of rainbow colors. I had the presence of mind to prepare a bowl, fill it with pure water, and set it on the ground in the path of the storm. I asked that this water be infused with the energies of this special cloud as it passed overhead. The cloud continued to move toward me, becoming darker in the center and more infused with pink light around its edges, and eventually passed directly over my position next to the lake. As it did, droplets of rain fell on the ground and into the bowl.

Healing Qualities—This essence cleanses and stabilizes the human electrical system. It is a powerful catalyst for release, and works especially well to discharge buildups of static energy that are being held in the body and in one's environment.

Solstice Storm is particularly helpful for those who live in areas of the planet where electrical storms and tornadoes are frequent, and who have difficulty dealing with the intense buildup of static electricity in the atmosphere that always precedes these storms.

This environmental essence can also be used to cleanse quartz crystals and other stones that have taken on static charges of energy through their use as healing tools.

I bless the old day setting, I honor the new day rising.
I open my eyes to the Love of the Sun;
in my heart we become one.

SOLSTICE SUN

Background Information—This essence was prepared during the "night" and early morning hours of June 21 and 22, as the midnight sun danced along the peaks of the Brooks Range in the northern interior of Alaska.

The area where this essence was prepared lies thirty-five miles north of the Arctic Circle, where there is constant daylight from April to late August. On the summer solstice, the longest day of the year, the sun barely dips below the tips of the mountain peaks, never fully disappearing from sight.

This essence was prepared by placing a bowl of water on the bank of the Koyukuk River in full view of the sun as it completed its decent from the northwest and began to rise again towards the northeast, an event lasting approximately four hours.

Healing Qualities—The essence of Solstice Sun contains the energy of the setting and rising sun—an embodiment of the completion of the old and the beginning of a new cycle of light.

Solstice Sun is a very transformational essence and can have a powerful effect on our ability to access and move energy through our physical bodies. It is often indicated for those who suffer from light deprivation, which is also known as Seasonal Affectedness Disorder.

This essence works by opening our hearts and the energy pathways in our bodies so that we can receive more light and make more efficient use of the energy contained within it.

This expansion in our ability to welcome light and energy into our bodies is also useful when we need to prepare ourselves for a peak experience—a kind of experience that we have never had before, or one that challenges us to expand the current parameters of our identity.

Solstice Sun is also an essence for integration. When it is taken during a peak or life changing experience, it will work on an elemental level to expand a person's energy system so that they can contain the fullness of the event as it unfolds. In this way, they are able to integrate the various aspects of the experience while they are still within the energetic or environmental matrix that is creating it.

All loss is gain.
I give and receive with constant, unyielding fluidity.

TIDAL FORCES

Background Information—This essence was prepared using fresh and salt water on Kachemak Bay during a full twenty-four hour, twenty-two-foot tidal cycle. I have included the following story of its preparation, which was edited from an account by Janice Schofield, because of its uniqueness and relevance to the healing qualities of the essence.

The men went to bed and I went off to the tide line with the glass bowl and water from Tutka Creek. I wandered along the shore by flashlight as it was dark and a snowy night, looking for a good altar for the bowl. I felt drawn to the sea cliffs, not knowing how high up the rocks the 4 a.m. tide (a 19.3 footer) would reach. I finally felt called to a rock shelf and placed the bowl in a small sea cave under the outreaching arms of an alder tree. At this point, the essence requested only pure water.

Dawn promised a fine day–new snow on the spruce, a smooth sea, and the essence fine but seeking sun and also a dash of fresh water from where little Jakolof Creek enters the bay, plus sea water from a deep pool. Later I was called to move the bowl again, to a flat rock exposed by the minus tide where ground fog was rolling on the beach. I reminded myself that I must move the bowl shortly as the tide would soon be returning.

Following lunch, I went to move the bowl, but it had vanished! Two feet of water covered the rock shelf. I kept searching the sea floor, hoping to at least retrieve the container. My heart experienced a "sinking" feeling and my first thought, sweeping in unbidden, was, "all loss is gain".

I returned to the house and shared the news with the crew. They discussed whether the bowl would float, and how long, with many theories circulating. Most thought it would quickly capsize in the cross currents but I went back to look again anyway. I descended to the beach and walked to tide line and there, afloat, coming directly to me, was the bowl, essence water still intact! I took one step into the bay and retrieved it, feeling deeply blessed by the tidal forces!

Such a unique essence, to have been carried about the bay in its bowl boat, swirling in the currents, dancing with the sea ducks. And still it continues, for a full cycle, high tide to high tide, low tide to low tide, a twenty-four hour dark/day/dark essence.

Yesterday at 9 p.m., as the sun was ebbing and tide flooding, I went to complete the preparation. I left the house in calm and fading sun, walked through a hailstorm, descended to the placid bay, poured the essence into the mother bottle, and returned to the house as waves began crashing surf sounds on the beach.

TIDAL FORCES

Healing Qualities—The quality of Alaska is one of drama and extremes, and Cook Inlet and Kachemak Bay are particularly dramatic because of the extreme tidal fluctuations that occur here.

The tide is the force of the sea, the rhythm of seasons and life. It is the giver and taker; it washes away the old and brings in the new. It persists in all seasons and in weather wild and calm.

This is an essence of rhythm and balance, of loss and gain, of adapting oneself to the swiftly changing currents of life. It helps one release the old and receive the new with constant and unyielding fluidity. It soothes and balances overly emotional, fiery states of being and helps wash away mental resistance to change, and to accepting what is in the present moment.

The Tidal Forces environmental essence is a balancer for extremes–for times of profound loss, times of darkness, times of being pressed against the sea cliffs by the tides of life. It helps us remember that the old is not being swept away against our will, but rather it is being removed because in our wisdom we have volunteered it.

Part Five

The
Alaskan Gem Elixirs

AQUAMARINE
Color—Light Blue
Correlations—5th, 6th Chakras, Mental Body

Indications—repetitive thoughts; overstimulated from studying, worrying and thinking; having difficulty letting go of thoughts and shifting into a meditative state of mind; not present for others because of preoccupation with mental activities.

Healing Qualities—increases the ability to achieve a neutral, serene state of mind; brings a calm, cooling clarity to an overactive mental body; releases blockages in the 5th and 6th chakras which create an excess of energy in the head and throat areas; helps create a mental oasis of cool, clear receptivity.

AVENTURINE
Color— Green
Correlations—3rd, 4th, 5th, 6th, 7th Chakras

Indications—lacking stamina and fortitude; wanting to quit when faced with obstacles, such as one's own limiting belief systems; fearful when facing the unknown; afraid to take risks in order to take the next step in life.

Healing Qualities—strengthens the central vertical axis which stabilizes us during expansion experiences; provides an energetic support structure that helps us move into and through new experiences with grace, stamina and perseverance; good for spiritual trailblazers and pioneers.

AZURITE
Color—Dark Blue
Correlations—5th Chakra, Spiritual Body

Indications—ungrounded communication, communicating from the head rather than through the body; struggling to communicate, straining to push words out; becoming physically depleted when speaking, teaching, or channeling information from nonphysical sources.

Healing Qualities—strengthens a nurturing connection between the feminine Earth forces and the 5th chakra; helps us communicate without depleting our physical vitality; helps us speak with authenticity, gentleness, and balance.

BLACK TOURMALINE
Color—Black
Correlations—1st Chakra, All Subtle Bodies

Indications—environmental toxicity; jet lag; overwhelmed by energies in the environment; oversensitive to televisions, computers, fluorescent lights, and other sources of environmental pollution; needing to detoxify on the physical, emotional, or mental levels but not knowing how to do it in a balanced way.

Healing Qualities—a precision tool for the release of toxic or stagnant energy held in the subtle bodies, the physical body, and the environment; absorbs inharmonious energies and exchanges them for fresh, clean energy; helps create the neutral space that is necessary before we can successfully invoke positive energies into our environment.

BLOODSTONE
Color—Green with Red Specks
Correlations—1st, 2nd, 4th Chakras, Etheric, Emotional Bodies

Indications—energetic stagnation and constipation; weak circulation of physical and emotional energy in the lower chakras and organs of the body; tendency to express emotional negativity; lacking emotional sensitivity and sympathy toward others.

Healing Qualities—brings a stronger flow of nourishing Earth energies into the 1st and 2nd chakras; stimulates the rapid release of energies that have been stuck in the lower chakras and in the emotional body; rebalances these energy centers after trauma or emotional upset.

BRAZILIAN AMETHYST
Color—Purple
Correlations—All Chakras, Etheric, Spiritual Bodies

Indications—over-identification with the gross, material aspects of life; separation from the spiritual realms; weak connection to one's higher self; resistance to bringing the spiritual into the physical.

Healing Qualities—transmutes energy from lower to higher vibratory rates; helps us create balance between our physical reality and our spiritual potential; promotes the lifting of perception from an overly material state; helps us bring the highest aspects of our spirituality into physical form.

BRAZILIAN QUARTZ
Color—Clear
Correlations—All Chakras and Subtle Bodies

Indications—tiredness, fatigue, low energy; weak energetic connection to the Earth; toxic or inharmonious energies in the aura; feeling out of touch with one or more aspects of self (physical, emotional, mental, spiritual), as though they were operating in different time zones; chakras out of alignment with each other.

Healing Qualities—the essence of cleansing white light; stimulates healing on all levels; cleanses, energizes and synchronizes the subtle bodies, the chakras, and the physical body to the Earth's natural vibration; brings a grounded, present time focus to the entire energy system.

CARNELIAN
Color—Yellow/Orange
Correlations—3rd Chakra, Etheric Body

Indications—burnout, fatigue, low energy during the day; weak sense of personal identity; giving in order to receive; addicted to helping others; seeking validation and energy from others rather than from within.

Healing Qualities—re-calibrates the 3rd chakra to draw life force energy through appropriate channels already present in the physical body and the aura; increases the etheric body's ability to access pranic energy; clears and energizes the nadirs–the subtle energy pathways between the etheric body and the meridians.

CHRYSOCOLLA
Color—Blue/Green
Correlation—4th Chakra

Indications—unresolved feelings of grief; heart closed down because of past experiences of loss; feeling a need to guard the heart against attack from others; believing that having an open heart will result in being hurt or wounded again; heart not energetically connected to the planet.

Healing Qualities—connects the heart chakra to the loving energy of the Earth; softens, opens and expands the inner dimensions of the heart chakra; increases flexibility and openness in the heart, mind and body to allow the vibration of love to flow; helps one experience the heart as a safe place to be.

CHRYSOPRASE
Color—Blue/Green
Correlations—4th Chakra, Etheric Body

Indications—alienation; not feeling at home on the planet or comfortable in nature; loving others but not the Earth; weak connection between the heart chakra and the Earth.

Healing Qualities—helps bring the heart chakra and the subtle bodies into harmonious union with the heart chakra of the Earth; develops the green, earthly dimension of the heart center; helps us accept the Earth as our home.

CITRINE
Color—Yellow
Correlations—All Chakras, Mental Body

Indications—mental confusion and distortion; lack of mental clarity and concentration; mental forces dominating physical and emotional aspects of self; difficulty determining what is in one's highest good; closed to higher sources of wisdom and inner knowing.

Healing Qualities—harmonizes the mental body with higher spiritual laws; increases access to Divine truth and intelligence; helps us translate what exists on the universal mental plane into usable information on the physical plane; amplifies qualities of concentration and centering; balances the intuitive and rational mind.

COVELLITE
Color—Dark Blue, Purple, Red
Correlations—5th, 6th Chakras, All Subtle Bodies

Indications—feeling unprotected and vulnerable; too easily stimulated by the energies of others, regardless of their intent; unsure of one's boundaries; unable to claim one's own space; feeling challenged by the environment.

Healing Qualities—brings strength, clarity and definition to the auric field; acts as a protective filter that encourages us to relax energetically, especially in the heart chakra area, thereby enhancing our ability to receive love and support from the environment.

DIAMOND
Color—Clear
Correlation—6th Chakra, Etheric, Emotional, Mental Bodies

Indications—life experience characterized by struggle; lack of clarity about the future; acting from a confused sense of what one is supposed to do; inability to make commitments; attached to personal will, to how "I" want it to be.

Healing Qualities—brings clarity to the 6th chakra; helps us see through illusion; harmonizes Divine and personal will; helps us activate personal will in its highest form; strengthens the ability to act in alignment with our Divine purpose.

EMERALD
Color—Green
Correlation—4th Chakra

Indications—fear of not being good enough to deserve being on the planet; weak or overly abstract connection to the feminine principle and to the Divine Mother; blocking the experience of love in the physical body because of fear; feeling unloved, cut off from one's center.

Healing Qualities—a universal heart cleanser and balancer; gently opens the heart to the unconditional love and nurturing of the Divine Mother; helps the heart become receptive to the highest qualities of the Divine feminine.

FLUORITE
Color—Purple
Correlations—7th Chakra, All Subtle Bodies

Indications—congestion, constriction, or stagnation of energy on any or all levels; rigidity, inflexibility; difficulty manifesting thoughts into action; hard to move one's focus from one area to another.

Healing Qualities—the "break-up" elixir; works to increase the circulation of energies in the physical body by breaking up and dispersing blockages in the etheric body; allows an increase of energy from the mental and emotional bodies to flow into the etheric and physical bodies.

FLUORITE COMBO
Colors—Yellow/Clear/Blue/Purple
Correlation—All Chakras & Mental, Emotional, Etheric Bodies

Indications—lacking focus or a clear sense of priorities when dealing with diverse issues that are coming up to be healed at the same time; feeling out of "synch" with one's inner processes; movement of energy between the subtle bodies and the physical body is not harmonious or synchronized.

Healing Qualities—synchronizes the movement of incoming and outgoing energy between the subtle bodies and the physical body; fine tunes our focus so that we can move through an issue or healing process with precision and balance.

GOLD
Color—Gold
Correlation—3rd Chakra

Indications—low self-esteem; weak sense of personal identity; little or no confidence in our ability to create; weak or uninspired masculine energies; difficulty manifesting wants and needs into physical reality; comparing our past accomplishments to other's.

Healing Qualities—brings strength, solidity, and balance to the 3rd chakra; helps us feel our inner value; enables us to access and bring forth into physical reality the highest aspects of our personal identity; helps us tap into our inner truth, joy, and wisdom as a source of creative power.

GREEN JASPER
Color—Green
Correlations—1st, 2nd, 3rd, 4th Chakras

Indications—ungrounded; lack of communication with the Earth; energy blocked in the lower chakras; inconsistent and uneven flow of sexual energy resulting from the shock or trauma of sexual abuse.

Healing Qualities—synchronizes body rhythms with earthly rhythms, especially when there has been a disruption to the natural flow; restores earthly sensuality and healthy sexuality; helps us reconnect to our instinctual natures; opens us to the energy and grace of the wild feminine.

HEMATITE
Color—Glossy Silver-Gray
Correlations—2nd, 3rd Chakras, Etheric, Emotional, Mental Bodies

Indications—unable to maintain one's boundaries while witnessing a highly charged emotional experience; getting swept away by other's negative feelings; emotionally co-dependent; having difficulty containing one's own emotional energy, especially in groups.

Healing Qualities—strengthens the energetic boundary between the mental and emotional bodies; promotes emotional independence rather than co-dependence; helps us maintain a state of compassionate detachment while witnessing an intense emotional experience in another; helps us contain our own emotional experiences in a clear way.

HERKIMER DIAMOND
Color—Clear
Correlations—All Chakras, Etheric, Emotional Bodies

Indications—psychic vision murky or undeveloped; low energy; unable to remember dreams; having confusing dreams full of chaotic imagery; difficulty bringing information from dream symbols into conscious under-standing.

Healing Qualities—a highly developed transmitter of white light; stimulates and amplifies healing at all levels; promotes clarity of vision; helps us regulate and fine tune the abilities of the 6th chakra; facilitates clarity during the dream state.

JADEITE JADE
Color—Green
Correlation—4th Chakra

Indications—agitated, upset; easily pulled out of center by intense experiences; making things harder or more involved than they need to be; unable to accept the way things are.

Healing Qualities—calming and centering; an enfolding vibration of peace, balance, and timeless simplicity; helps us live in the moment, in our center, with an awareness and acceptance of our true and essential selves.

KUNZITE
Color—Transparent Pink
Correlations—4th, 7th Chakras

Indications—feelings of guilt and embarrassment concerning one's past actions; out of touch with one's angelic presence; lack of awareness of the angelic love, guidance, and support that is available; heart closed to the flow of spiritual love coming into the body.

Healing Qualities—opens the heart to an awareness of one's angelic presence; anchors the reality of angelic support into the body and one's environment; helps one experience the spiritual love of the angelic kingdom in the heart, in the moment; develops the higher octave of the heart chakra.

LAPIS LAZULI
Color—Blue
Correlations—5th, 6th Chakras

Indications—unable to hear or understand guidance and information from higher sources; having difficulty communicating clearly with others, especially about information that one has received from these sources; overwhelmed by the amount of information coming in.

Healing Qualities—opens and regulates channels of communication; connects the hearing ability of the 5th chakra with the innate knowing and wisdom of the 6th chakra; strengthens our ability to speak with the authority of the higher self; helps us communicate information of a higher nature in a clear and understandable way; great for speakers, teachers, intuitive practitioners and writers.

MALACHITE
Color—Green
Correlations—1st, 2nd, 3rd, 4th Chakras, Etheric Body

Indications—weak energetic connection to the physical world; forward movement in life held up because of a lack of grounding; emotional, mental, and physical aspects working at cross-purposes with each other.

Healing Qualities—helps ground all parts of the energy field to the Earth; aligns and harmonizes the four levels of being; supports the energetic unity of the body/soul connection in all circumstances; helps one get it together and keep it together when moving through transition and transformation.

MOLDAVITE
Color—Dark Green
Correlations—4th Chakra, Spiritual Body

Indications—caught up in the dualities of here or there, now or then; going out of the body for information rather than staying present to receive it; feeling separate and out of touch, especially with the higher self.

Healing Qualities—connectedness; helps us stay present in the body, in the moment, and access the information and perspective we need to better express our earthly potential; an energetic window to universal perspective and higher dimensional reality.

MONTANA RHODOCHROSITE
Color—Pink
Correlation—4th Chakra

Indications—heart closed down after an abrupt loss or separation from a partner or loved one; feeling unsafe in the heart and wanting to escape into the head; fearful of powerful emotions; unable to process emotions fully in the heart.

Healing Qualities—brings strength and solidity to the heart chakra; restores wholeness to the heart after an experience of great pain and suffering; clears distortion, fear, confusion and chaos from the heart; clarifies intent and promotes courageous, heart-centered action.

MOONSTONE
Color—Milky White
Correlations—2nd Chakra, Emotional Body

Indications—heightened psychic sensitivity during menstruation; touchy, edgy, over-reactive; emotional energy blocked and difficult to express in a clear way; lack of sensitivity and intuitive awareness in men and women; hard edged persona.

Healing Qualities—helps us move into an authentic feeling space rather than an over-reactive one; cleanses and circulates energy in the emotional body; helps us complete emotional cycles; calming, soothing, and nurturing; balances and harmonizes psychic sensitivity during menstruation.

OPAL
Color—Multicolored
Correlations—All Chakras and Subtle Bodies

Indications—burned out; insomnia from overuse of the mental forces; tiredness that is not helped by sleep; excessive use of the fire element; depletion of certain energy frequencies in the chakras and subtle bodies; vital energy reserves used up; emotional exhaustion.

Healing Qualities—recharges the chakras with a full spectrum of luminous colors; helps us rejuvenate spent emotional and mental forces; counteracts the depletion of color frequencies in the aura; replenishes our creative energies; helps us learn to use the fire element in a balanced way.

ORANGE CALCITE
Color—Orange
Correlation—2nd Chakra, Etheric Body

Indications—sadness, depression of unknown origin, lack of joy in physical life; lethargy, feeling weighted down, no creative spark; unable to see the positive side of life in everyday situations; greatly affected by seasonal fluctuations of sunlight and darkness.

Healing Qualities—penetrating, uplifting, energizing, warming; amplifies one's ability to assimilate light at the cellular level of the body; opens the heart to the energy of the Sun; dispels darkness and grief; helps one feel joy and a sense of creative connectedness to the physical realm.

PEARL
Color—Milky White
Correlations—Etheric, Emotional, Mental Bodies

Indications—irritated by one's own problems and difficulties, especially those manifesting in the physical body in a painful way; lacking understanding and compassion for one's own healing processes.

Healing Qualities—helps one process and dissolve layers of irritation that have built up in the mental and emotional bodies and are seen in the physical body as hardness and inflexibility; helps turn antagonism toward oneself and criticism or judgment of one's illness into acceptance and understanding.

PERIDOT
Color—Light Green
Correlations—4th Chakra, Etheric, Emotional Bodies

Indications—trepidation, fear, and insecurity during the beginning phase of any new experience; projections of failure when attempting to learn or do something new; feeling unprotected in that space where the known has fallen away, and the new has not yet become manifest.

Healing Qualities—the stone of new beginnings; provides support and protection for any new cycle of growth or experience; helps us create a fresh, clear space in the heart for something new to be born into; stabilizes the heart and subtle bodies during the incubation period of new ideas and creative projects; supports deep experiences of healing and transformation where there is a rebirth of awareness and energy.

PYRITE
Color—Metallic Gold
Correlations—2nd, 3rd Chakras, Etheric Body

Indications—easily influenced by others, especially members of one's peer group; unable to make decisions or stand up for oneself; involved in relationships that are not in one's highest good; tension and instability from not being true to oneself.

Healing Qualities—strengthens self-esteem and self-trust, especially with regard to group dynamics and peer pressure; helps one build an energetic foundation in life based on one's highest personal truth; solidifies values, helps one be true to oneself.

RHODOCHROSITE
Color—Pink/Red
Correlations—2nd, 4th Chakras, Etheric and Emotional Bodies

Indications—deep trauma and emotional pain in the heart; unable to make intimate connections with others; shut down emotionally or sexually as a result of being abused; feeling cut off and alienated from the physical world.

Healing Qualities—increases energy, balance, and stability in the heart chakra and in the physical body; soothing and nurturing to the heart during and after deep healing and transformation; heals the effects of abuse in the heart so that the corresponding trauma can be released from the physical body.

RHODOLITE GARNET
Color—Red
Correlations—1st, 2nd Chakras, Etheric Body

Indications—emotionally and energetically disconnected from parts of the body that are in pain or have been injured or operated on; parts of the body won't heal or return to their normal level of function; poor circulation in certain areas of the body.

Healing Qualities—increases one's ability to inhabit the physical body; helps one reconnect energetically with parts of the body that have been traumatized; rebuilds the etheric web in areas disrupted by injury or surgery so that one can draw in the forces that are needed to complete the healing process.

ROSE QUARTZ
Color—Pink
Correlations—4th Chakra, Etheric, Emotional Bodies

Indications—pain held in the heart from traumatic events in one's past; heart closed down because of not being nurtured as a child; difficulty initiating and maintaining intimate contact with others; inner child not receiving nurturing energy from the adult; lack of compassion for others.

Healing Qualities—develops all dimensions of the heart chakra; helps one anchor love into the physical body through the heart center; helps one connect to and nurture one's inner child; opens, strengthens, and stabilizes the heart forces so an individual is able to maintain intimacy with oneself, others, and the planet.

RUBY
Color—Dark Red
Correlations—1st, 4th Chakras

Indications—unresolved survival issues blocking energy flow between the Earth and the 1st chakra; constipation of energies in the lower chakras and organs of the body; ambivalence about being present in the physical body; tendency to disconnect from the body during times of chaos and upheaval.

Healing Qualities—cleanses, balances, and energizes the 1st chakra; opens the lower chakras to a stronger flow of life force energy from the Earth; supports one's ability to ground spiritual and mental energy into the physical body, especially during times of intense transformation.

RUTILATED QUARTZ
Color—Clear with Gold-colored filaments
Correlations—All Chakras, Mental Body

Indications—overwhelmed by the amount of energy and information coming in from nonphysical sources; distortion, confusion, and/or lack of focus and clarity during meditation or attunement; unable to understand or integrate information and guidance from the higher self.

Healing Qualities—promotes precision alignment with higher sources of energy and information; helps us develop and physically stabilize the ability to access, focus, synthesize, and express information from the spiritual realms.

SAPPHIRE
Color—Blue
Correlations—5th, 6th, Chakras, Spiritual Body

Indications—feeling unsupported for being on the Earth; unaware of life purpose; lack of inspiration and commitment; feeling out of touch and out of place; unwilling or unable to take responsibility for why one has incarnated.

Healing Qualities—helps us connect to the energetic support we need to do the work we came here to do; helps us move to a deeper level of inner work and life experience; promotes loyalty to action that serves our highest truth; strengthens commitment to Divine purpose.

SAPPHIRE/RUBY
Color—Blue/Pink
Correlations—1st, 4th, 5th, 6th Chakras, All Subtle Bodies

Indications—weak body/soul connection; lack of alignment between spiritual and physical bodies due to past injury or debilitating disease; difficulty integrating awareness of life purpose into practical, heart-centered action.

Healing Qualities—helps anchor the qualities of devotion, responsibility, and loyalty firmly into the heart; gently facilitates the integration of higher purpose into day-to-day physical reality; helps us balance spiritual responsibility with physical ability; helps us receive nurturing through the fulfillment of Divine responsibilities.

SCEPTER AMETHYST
Color—Transparent Purple
Correlations—All Chakras, All Subtle Bodies

Indications— lacking spiritual perseverance; unable to take an active stand for what one believes; in a position of authority but lacking in spiritual leadership qualities; one's experience of the spiritual realm is abstract rather than direct.

Healing Qualities—gives strength and support to follow one's spiritual path; opens and prepares the 7th chakra to receive energy from the higher chakras; awakens our highest spiritual potential; helps us embody a higher level of spiritual authority and leadership qualities.

SMOKY QUARTZ
Color—Transparent Smoky Gray
Correlations—All Chakras, All Subtle Bodies

Indications—ungrounded, agitated; disassociated from the physical body; body feels out of synch with the surrounding environment; detoxification happening at too rapid a pace for the physical body to keep up with; jet lag.

Healing Qualities—grounding and calming; synchronizes body energy with Earth energy; regulates and stabilizes the detoxification of unwanted energies from the physical and subtle bodies; cleanses and re-calibrates body energies during and after travel.

SPECTROLITE
Color—Steel Blue with multicolored highlights
Correlations—6th Chakra, Etheric Body

Indications—seeing with the eyes, but not with the heart; low creative spark; unable to sense the deeper meaning of life's events; cloudy, dark, or outdated perspective on life; tendency to see the negative in each situation.

Healing Qualities—renews and refreshes one's perspective; helps one contact deeper levels of meaning in life's events; helps one see the magnificent in the mundane, the Divine in the ordinary; bathes and nourishes the entire energy system with full spectrum light.

STAR SAPPHIRE
Color—Blue/Purple
Correlations—5th, 6th, Chakras, All Subtle Bodies

Indications—lacking trust in the universe; difficulty making the right choices and connections in one's life; overconcern for the smallest details of one's process; unable to connect energetically with information about one's higher purpose.

Healing Qualities—promotes trust in the universe; helps focus one's awareness on what is necessary for the soul's progression in life; helps one make energetic and physical connections that support the realization of one's destiny.

SUGALITE
Color—Deep Purple
Correlations—6th, 7th Chakras, Spiritual Body

Indications—living with a highly refined or intellectual concept of what the spiritual realm must be like, rather than a grounded, physically embodied experience of what it is; believing that one must go outside oneself to truly experience spiritual support.

Healing Qualities—brings depth and a physical richness to one's spiritual life; helps one learn to receive spiritual support easily and gracefully; helps one physically manifest a warmer, more feminine quality of spirituality.

TIGER'S EYE
Color—Brown/Gold
Correlations—2nd, 3rd Chakras, Emotional, Etheric Body

Indications—loses sense of self-identity when dealing with powerful emotions, whether generated by the self or by others; reacts rather than responds; often angry or jealous; strongly affected by the energy of others; takes things personally.

Healing Qualities—self-empowerment; helps one maintain a strong sense of self-identity when dealing with powerful emotions such as anger, fear and jealousy; strengthens the energetic boundary between one's emotional experiences and one's true nature.

TOPAZ
Color—Transparent Gold
Correlation—3rd Chakra

Indications—unable to take decisive action that supports one's true self; confused sense of personal identity; tries to connect to others for energy in inappropriate ways; identifies more with others than with the self.

Healing Qualities—clears energy blockages in the 3rd chakra; strengthens our ability to act decisively from a clear sense of personal identity and Divine purpose; helps us access appropriate sources of universal energy.

TURQUOISE
Color—Sky Blue
Correlations—5th Chakra, Spiritual Body

Indications—lack of reverence for the Earth; no gratitude for nature's gifts; too busy to honor the sacredness of life; taking without asking or giving something back; living a life without soul.

Healing Qualities—cleanses and deepens our connection to the Soul of the Earth; attunes our energy field to the ancient wisdom and sacredness inherent in all of life; helps us live a life of simplicity, full of gratitude and reverence for All.

WATERMELON TOURMALINE
Color—Pink/Green
Correlation—4th Chakra

Indications—disharmony between the masculine and feminine aspects of the self; lack of balance between giving and receiving; difficulty expressing love for others, or receiving love from others.

Healing Qualities—balances the universal polarities of yin and yang; harmonizes the dynamic and magnetic (giving and receiving) qualities of love; helps us ground spiritual and angelic qualities of love into the heart and physical body.

Part Six

Alaskan Combination Formulas
&
Sacred Space Sprays

Alaskan Combination Formulas

The Alaskan Combination Formulas are unique blends of flower, gem and environmental essences. They possess a special co-creative synergy that is only possible when healing energies from the flower, mineral, and elemental kingdoms are combined through focused intent.

These formulas were born out of many years of research, observation, and feedback received from clients and therapists from around the world.

Soul Support™

Cattail Pollen • Chalice Well • Cotton Grass • Fireweed • Labrador Tea Malachite • River Beauty • Ruby • White Fireweed

Soul Support (formerly Emergency Care) brings strength and stability during emergencies, stress, trauma and transformation, while providing support to rejuvenate and restore balance on all levels. Following is a list of situations where this formula has proven helpful:
- Accidents involving injury, shock, and trauma
- Emotional catharsis and violent outbursts
- Fear of flying
- Motion sickness
- Before, during, and after visits to the dentist
- After a fight, argument, or disagreement
- After receiving shocking news such as a death in the family
- Divorce, job changes, and moving to a new place
- Post traumatic stress
- Before and immediately after surgery and during recovery
- Abrupt and major changes in plans
- In an animal shelter
- In wild animal rescue and rehabilitation work
- When transplanting in the garden and with cut flowers
- For any transition, challenge, or initiation

Special Instructions: During times of acute stress take four drops directly from the bottle under the tongue, or put 4-6 drops in a glass of water or juice and sip frequently. If the person needing Soul Support cannot drink, several drops of the stock concentrate can be rubbed on their lips, temples, or on the pulse points of the body. Dosage bottles can be made up ahead of time by adding four drops of stock to a one-ounce dropper bottle, filled with 75% water and 25% percent brandy or vegetable glycerine.

Soul Support can be used by the whole family. For children, dilute the stock drops in water if giving orally. Animals may take the stock directly, or it can be sprayed on or around their bodies. This formula should not be used as a substitute for qualified medical care or intervention.

Travel Ease™

White Violet • Yarrow • Covellite • Black Tourmaline • Smoky Quartz

The Travel Ease combination is specifically designed to ease the negative effects of air travel, including what is commonly referred to as jet lag.

This formula supports the establishment and maintenance of functional energy boundaries. If you are environmentally sensitive and have difficulty being confined in small, constricted spaces for long periods of time, Travel Ease will help you feel as though you have all the personal space you need, even on a crowded flight. Use Travel Ease:

• To help you maintain the overall integrity of your energy field, which is challenged by electromagnetic radiation produced by the plane's electronics and wiring, and by the noise and vibration generated by the plane during flight.

• To promote the ongoing release of any toxic or unwanted energies that you absorb during your flight. This accumulation of "airborne" pollutants in the auric field during a long flight is one of the main factors contributing to jet lag.

• To help you maintain your grounding during the flight by keeping your body energies synchronized and aligned with the Earth's energy field as you move from one location to another. For many, the disorientation that comes from traveling to new places and from moving through multiple time zones is the worst part of the traveling experience. Travel Ease helps you avoid it by constantly updating your energetic relationship with the Earth as you travel, so that when you arrive at your final destination, you are truly there, energetically as well as physically.

Special Instructions: For maximum effectiveness, begin taking this combination several days before your flight, at least three times during the flight, and for a few days after you reach your destination. For extended travel, such as an overseas flight, the formula should be taken every hour you are airborne. The easiest way is to add several drops of stock concentrate to your water bottle and sip from it at regular intervals.

Fireweed Combo™

Fireweed • River Beauty • White Fireweed • Dwarf Fireweed

Fireweed Combo supports the processes of transformation, transition, and change. It can be used to prepare for a transformational experience of any kind, but it is especially useful when you are in the middle of an intense process and need extra support to get through it. Fireweed Combo enables you to access the support you need to face your fears, let go of your resistance, and open to the process as it moves forward to completion. Using this formula will help you:

• Strengthen your grounding connection to the Earth, so your energy system will be more stable and better able to cope with change.

• Break up and move out old energy patterns that are being held in your body.

• Identify and release suppressed emotional energies that are attached to the patterns you are opening to release.

• Stay engaged with the transformative process until you have resolved all of the issues that are connected to it.

• Reconnect with the desired levels of joy and happiness that are your birthright.

Special Instructions: The Fireweed Combo formula can be taken internally or added to your bath whenever you need additional support to make it through a period of intense transformation or change.

Lighten Up™

Carnelian • Grass of Parnassus • Orange Calcite • Solstice Sun

Lighten Up is a combination formula designed to increase your ability to embody light. Its overall effect is to uplift, energize, inspire and nourish.

Lighten Up was designed specifically for people who suffer from light deprivation. This condition may be present because of where they live (in the extreme northern or southern latitudes or in a dark house or apartment), or because of the quality of their energy system (energy pathways blocked or undeveloped). This formula is also helpful for those who are depressed, caught in negative patterns or situations, or feel cut off in any way from their inner sources of light.

The ingredients in Lighten Up work on three main levels. The first is to open and cleanse the chakras so you can draw more life force energy through appropriate channels already present in your energy system. The second is to cleanse and expand the energy pathways in your physical body. This includes amplifying your ability to assimilate light at the cellular level. The third is to strengthen your ability to integrate experience, thereby increasing the amount of energy that can flow through your body and life.

The primary action of Lighten Up is to help you become more efficient at accessing and using the light that is available to you. This will enable you to enjoy a more consistent and sustained energy flow regardless of seasonal fluctuations of sunlight or other limiting factors in your environment.

Use the Lighten Up formula:
- When you are fatigued or feel a lack of energy on the physical level.
- For Seasonal Affectedness Disorder.
- In the classroom, when you are getting tired of sitting and receiving information.
- With animals that are kept inside for long periods of time during the cold winter months.
- On plants, to give them extra light and energy during short winter days.
- When you are doing Space Clearing and want to enhance the qualities of light and energy in the environment you are working with.

Special Instructions: The Lighten Up formula can be taken internally or added to your bath whenever you feel the need for more light and energy. It is also very effective when sprayed on the body and in your environment. Mist it into your house or office after it has been cleansed with our Purification formula.

Purification™

Black Tourmaline • Fireweed • Portage Glacier • Sweetgrass

Purification is a formula designed to cleanse and purify your home and work environments and your personal energy field. It can be utilized to break up and cleanse stagnant patterns of energy on any level. Use Purification when you need to:

• Release toxic energy from the mind, emotions, and body.

• Release old ingrained habits that are no longer useful, necessary, or contributing to your well-being.

• Break up unhealthy patterns of energy in an environment where there has been addiction, depression, or abuse.

• Revitalize, balance and stimulate the renewal of energy on all levels or your energy system.

• Create a pure and protected inner space when you find yourself in crowded or polluted surroundings.

• Purify and recharge the atmosphere where there is stagnant energy–the first step in the Space Clearing process.

Special Instructions: Purification can be taken internally whenever you need additional support during a fast, or any cleansing or detoxifying process. Putting drops of Purification in an indoor fountain is a great way to constantly purify and revitalize a room. This formula can also be added to wash water to elevate household chores to a sacred activity.

Guardian™

Covellite • Devil's Club • Round-Leaf Orchid • Stone Circle White Violet • Yarrow

Guardian is a formula that helps you create a powerful force-field of protection in your aura. It invokes positive, harmonious energies that help you claim your space, maintain your grounding, and feel the protection of strong, healthy boundaries. This combination is helpful when you:

• Are ambivalent about being present in your body and on the Earth, because you don't feel safe or protected.

• Have just moved into a new neighborhood and are having difficulty grounding into your new situation.

• Are unable to embody your sensitivity in a practical and easy way because of a lack of functional boundaries.

• Are over-reactive to influences in your environment.

• Feel tired or run down and need to rest and nurture yourself, but can't seem to create the space to do it.

• Are having difficulty staying in your heart in times of discomfort.

• Are doing healing work such as massage, reiki and counseling that requires you to be in the personal energy space of others.

• Work around computers and other electromagnetic equipment or in toxic environments.

• Are doing Space Clearing, Interior Alignment, or similar work that requires you to enter into another person's living or working space.

• Have children that need to strengthen their emotional and energetic boundaries so they will be less reactive to stressful family dynamics.

• Want to become the source of your own protection.

Special Instructions: The Guardian formula can be taken internally whenever you feel the need for more protection. It can also be added to creams and lotions and applied to those areas of the body that need extra support.

Calling All Angels™

Angelica • Chalice Well • Chiming Bells • Kunzite

Calling All Angels is an invocation formula that helps you contact the love, guidance, and protection of the angelic realm. It brings a very soft and serene energy into your heart, physical body and environment. Use it to:

• Strengthen the knowledge that you are guided, supported, and protected by the angels.

• Come into a stronger awareness of your own angelic nature.

• Experience the love of the angelic kingdom in your physical body.

• Bring the essence of joy and peace back in to your life.

• Make a stronger connection to the Divine feminine.

• Create a sacred and protected space for sleeping and dreaming.

Special Instructions: Take internally or add to the bath whenever you want to invoke the loving energy of the angels. Add to your body lotions and creams when you feel the need for some additional pampering, and to your massage oil for a heavenly bodywork session.

Sacred Space Sprays™

Jane Bell and Steve Johnson have co-created three new **Sacred Space Sprays** for *Space Clearing*, an ancient practice brought to life by Denise Linn in her book <u>Sacred Space</u>. Jane is a graduate of Denise's Interior Alignment program and practices *Space Clearing* professionally, helping people to create healing environments.

We began with our popular Purification, Guardian, and Calling All Angels formulas and added custom blends of the highest quality essential oils. Each blend contains oils that were specifically chosen on the basis of their therapeutic qualities. These oils enhance the function of each combination and make it possible for the healing energies of the essences to stay present in the environment for long periods of time.

These water based sprays also contain an emulsifier extracted from natural vegetable oils. This product encapsulates the essential oils, enabling them to be evenly and fully dispersed into the air.

We created these sprays to address the challenge of maintaining our health in this crowded and fast paced world. Stagnant and toxic energies accumulate in our living and working environments from computers and other electrical equipment, pollution, emotional upsets, illness, clutter, and even from the energies of previous occupants. Over time these disharmonious energies can have a draining effect on our physical vitality, relationships, productivity, creativity, prosperity, and general well-being. You can cleanse your surroundings of these unwanted toxins and bring in the fresh, elementally infused energies of nature by utilizing our **Sacred Space Sprays** along with the simple and straightforward techniques of *Space Clearing*.

These sprays were designed to help you evolve from a position of being at the mercy of your surroundings to having a positive effect on them. Our vision is to help people create clear and vibrant living and working environments which will benefit everyone who enters them. The apartments, houses and buildings in which we live and work can become beacons of light that radiate out and positively transform our neighborhoods, cities, countries and the world.

Using the Sacred Space Sprays

(1) Begin to create Sacred Space by centering yourself and saying a prayer of gratitude. State that your intention is to clear stagnant, inharmonious

energies from the environment and replace them with positive, uplifting, life affirming energies from nature and the angelic kingdoms. Call in the elements of air, earth, fire and water to enhance and add power to the process.

(2) To cleanse the environment you are working in, spray **Purification** around the room, paying extra attention to the corners and any areas that feel heavy or dense. Continue in each room you are Space Clearing.

(3) When the space feels clear, you are ready to invoke fresh, new patterns of energy using one or both of our invocation sprays:

• Spray **Guardian** around the room or building when you want to invoke the energies of calm, stability and security. **Guardian** sets a grounded and radiant energy into the space that helps each person who enters move into their center and maintain a connection to the source of their protection–their own inner light.

• Use **Calling All Angels** when you want to attract the nurturing, uplifting and joyful qualities of the angelic kingdom. This spray brings a very sacred and peaceful energy into the space. Children love to spray their rooms before sleeping to create a feeling of protection and to insure a deep, restful slumber.

(4) To complete the process, give thanks and ask to close your connection with the forces of air, earth, fire and water. Notice the vibrancy and freshness of your environment and how good this feels!

We recommend using these sprays on a regular basis to cleanse, energize and protect your personal energy field and maintain the clarity of your home and work environments. They are also very useful when you are traveling. Spray your hotel room when you arrive and your rental car when you pick it up. We hope you will enjoy using the **Sacred Space Sprays** as much as we did co-creating them, and we would love to hear about your experiences with them!

Part Seven

Cross-Reference of
Healing Qualities

Abundance

unconditional acceptance of abundance—*Bog Blueberry*
releasing mental limitations to the experience of abundance on all levels—
Blueberry Pollen
increasing the feeling of inner worth—*Columbine, Gold, Lace Flower,*
Sphagnum Moss

Abuse

releasing the cellular impact of abuse—*Black Tourmaline, Tundra*
Twayblade, White Fireweed
recovering from experiences of emotional abuse—*River Beauty, Sweetgale*
healing and releasing the effects of abuse on the body—*Cotton Grass,*
Northern Lady's Slipper, Rhodochrosite, Soul Support
healing the impact of sexual abuse—*Balsam Poplar, Cotton Grass, River*
Beauty, White Fireweed

Acceptance

of the oneness of all creation—*Green Fairy Orchid*
of support, regardless of the form it comes clothed in—*Spiraea*
of the impulses of spirit—*Jacob's Ladder*
of one's unique and personal beauty—*Columbine*
of what is in the present moment—*Jadeite Jade, Tidal Forces*
turning self-judgment into acceptance—*Pearl, Sphagnum Moss*

Addictions

addicted to helping others in return for their energy—*Carnelian*
helps one tap into appropriate sources of energy—*Topaz*
difficulty letting go of—*Labrador Tea, Opal*

Agitation

calms emotional agitation—*Jadeite Jade, Tidal Forces, Soul Support*

Alignment

between physical, emotional, mental, and spiritual aspects of being—
Malachite
with higher sources of energy and information—*Rutilated Quartz, Topaz*
with the power of one's personal truth—*Cattail Pollen*
deep realignment with one's highest purpose in life—*Ladies' Tresses*

Alignment (cont)

restores alignment between the spiritual and physical bodies—*Ruby, Sapphire/Ruby*

energetic alignment with Divine purpose—*Diamond, Paper Birch, Sapphire, Star Sapphire*

Ambivalence

about being on the planet—*Chrysoprase, Shooting Star*

about being present in the physical body—*Rainbow Glacier, Ruby, Devil's Club*

Anger

understanding and releasing anger through the heart—*Blue Elf Viola*

Animals / Animal Care

treating shock and trauma in animals—*Fireweed, River Beauty, Sweetgrass, White Fireweed, Soul Support*

healing the effects of abuse—*Balsam Poplar, Cotton Grass, Tundra Twayblade*

support for the newborn—*Green Bells of Ireland, Peridot, Spiraea, White Violet*

helps establish a nurturing bond between mothers and their offspring—*Grove Sandwort, Pineapple Weed*

helps humans and animals release their fear of other animals—*Bog Rosemary, Monkshood, Soapberry*

supports the healing process after surgery—*Cotton Grass, Northern Lady's Slipper, Opal, Rhodolite Garnet*

Attachment

releasing inappropriate ego attachment—*Round-Leaved Sundew*

releasing attachment to pain—*Cotton Grass*

releasing one's attachment to old emotions—*River Beauty*

releasing attachment to the form our support must take before we are willing to accept it—*Spiraea*

moving beyond one's attachment to distraction—*Bunchberry*

letting go of inappropriate emotional attachment to others—*Sweetgale*

letting go of attachment to the form of what has been—*Glacier River, Greenland Icecap*

Attunement

to the needs of the plant kingdom—*Moschatel*
to very subtle levels of physical manifestation—*Northern Twayblade*
to the sounds and energies present in nature—*Cassandra*
to the intelligence existing in nature—*Green Bells of Ireland*
to the collective consciousness of the planet—*Black Spruce*
to the wisdom of the higher self—*Brazilian Amethyst, White Spruce*
focusing and refining one's attunement to the plant kingdom—*Green Bog Orchid*
helps one access, focus, and synthesize information during an attunement—*Rutilated Quartz*

Authority

helps one establish a new core of spiritual authority—*Scepter Amethyst*
helps one accept the authority of the higher self—*Hairy Butterwort, Jacob's Ladder, Sunflower*

Awareness

of information from beyond our normal range of perception—*Alder*
of emotional tension held in the muscle tissues of the body—*Dandelion*
of subtle energy flows in and around the body—*Lady's Slipper*
of illusion—*Bladderwort*
of how one's energy affects others—*One-Sided Wintergreen*
of support and guidance from higher realms—*Chalice Well, Hairy Butterwort, Kunzite*
of one's Divine identity—*Monkshood, Scepter Amethyst, Sugalite*
of support and nurturing from nature—*Emerald, Grove Sandwort, Pineapple Weed, Spiraea*
of the omnipresence of light—*Single Delight*
of one's true self—*Tamarack, Topaz*
of one's life purpose—*Ladies' Tresses, Paper Birch*
of one's highest spiritual potential—*Scepter Amethyst*
clearing and focusing one's awareness in order to deepen one's connection with the plant kingdom—*Comandra, Green Bog Orchid, Northern Twayblade*

Balance

in the expression of the masculine, in men or women—*Sunflower*

Balance (cont.)

in communication—*Azurite*

of logic and intuition—*White Spruce*

of masculine and feminine expressions of power—*Sitka Spruce Pollen*

between the heart and the mind—*Lamb's Quarters, Wild Rhubarb*

between the celestial and the physical—*Rainbow Glacier, Sapphire/Ruby, Shooting Star*

Balancing

extreme states of energy—*Labrador Tea*

intuition, thought, and emotion in the present moment—*White Spruce*

activity and rest, evolution and being—*Opium Poppy*

listening and speaking skills—*Twinflower*

one's personal power with the power of nature—*Soapberry*

power and gentleness—*Sitka Spruce Pollen*

sexual energy in the body—*Balsam Poplar*

male and female energies in the heart—*Green Fairy Orchid*

magnetic and dynamic, giving and receiving—*Watermelon Tourmaline*

overly emotionalized, fiery states of being—*Tidal Forces*

lower chakra energies—*Bloodstone, Green Jasper, Ruby*

Boundaries

strengthening the boundary between the emotional and mental bodies—*Bunchberry, Hematite*

giving strength and definition to one's energy field   *Covellite, Yarrow, Guardian*

creating boundaries in alignment with one's highest truth—*One-Sided Wintergreen*

creating functional energy boundaries through Divine trust and a strong connection with one's higher self—*Monkshood, White Violet*

maintaining strong boundaries when confined in small spaces, such as airplanes—*Travel Ease*

Centering

helps one hold their center during intense experiences—*Hematite, Jadeite Jade, Labrador Tea*

Childbirth

support for the mother and child during and immediately after the birth—*Grove Sandwort, Spiraea, Peridot*

release of pelvic tension during childbirth—*Balsam Poplar*

release of trauma from the birth experience, regardless of one's present age—*Northern Lady's Slipper*

helping the newborn feel welcome on the Earth—*Green Bells of Ireland, Shooting Star*

support for moving from one stage of delivery to the next—*Hairy Butterwort, Sticky Geranium*

Clarity

of dreams—*Herkimer Diamond*

of purpose—*Diamond, Ladies' Tresses, Paper Birch*

of vision—*Herkimer Diamond*

translating clarity of perception into appropriate action—*Alder*

hearing and speaking from a place of inner clarity—*Twinflower*

mental clarity, especially during emotionally demanding situations—*Bunchberry*

emotional clarity in communication—*Sweetgale*

brings clarity to an overactive mental body—*Aquamarine, Citrine*

Cleansing

the channel of communication between the heart and the mind—*Wild Rhubarb*

the etheric body—*Carnelian, Fluorite, Fluorite Combo, Sweetgrass*

the body's electrical system—*Solstice Storm*

old energy patterns from the body—*Fireweed, Greenland Icecap, Purification, Sitka Burnet*

one's connection with the Soul of the Earth—*Turquoise*

core cleansing and re-patterning of the heart—*Northern Lights*

toxic energy from the mind, emotions, and physical body—*Black Tourmaline, Greenland Icecap, Portage Glacier, Purification, Smoky Quartz*

chaotic and confused energy from the heart—*Emerald, Foxglove, Montana Rhodochrosite, Rhodochrosite*

emotional energy from the lower chakras—*Bloodstone, Ruby, Sweetgale*

Communication

between mother and child—*Grove Sandwort, Pineapple Weed*

between different levels of consciousness—*Horsetail*

between the heart and mind—*Wild Rhubarb*

between people and the Earth—*Brazilian Quartz, Cassandra, Pineapple Weed*

with one's higher self—*Golden Corydalis, Scepter Amethyst, Tundra Rose, White Violet*

with the plant kingdom—*Comandra, Green Bells of Ireland, Green Bog Orchid, Moschatel*

with the animal kingdom—*Horsetail*

with one's own sources of guidance and support—*Hairy Butterwort, Kunzite, Sugalite*

from a place of inner calm and neutrality—*Twinflower*

developing body/mind communication—*Dandelion*

improving emotional communication in relationships—*Hematite, Sweetgale*

precision alignment with inter-dimensional sources of information—*Rutilated Quartz*

enhances one's ability to communicate with vitality, authenticity and gentleness—*Azurite*

clears channels of communication in the 5th chakra—*Lapis Lazuli*

Compassion

through forgiveness—*Mountain Wormwood*

for all beings through loving kindness—*Bleeding Heart*

helps one develop compassion for one's own healing processes—*Green Bog Orchid, Pearl, Sphagnum Moss*

developing compassion for oneself and others through self-acceptance—*Alpine Azalea*

Completion

of the past on all levels—*Sitka Burnet*

of cycles of learning and experience—*Grass of Parnassus, Polar Ice*

of cycles of healing on the etheric level—*Sweetgrass*

of cycles of learning without the creation of crisis or illness—*Hairy Butterwort*

of emotional cycles—*Moonstone, River Beauty*

Confidence

from knowing one's abilities—*Tamarack*
from knowing one's purpose in life—*Paper Birch, Sapphire*

Confusion

clears mental confusion and distortion—*Bunchberry, Citrine*
clears confusing dream imagery—*Herkimer Diamond*
clears confusion and chaos from the heart after a traumatic experience—
Montana Rhodochrosite, Rose Quartz, Tundra Twayblade

Consciousness

opening to wisdom contained in the collective consciousness of the
planet—*Black Spruce, White Spruce*
communicating with other levels of consciousness—*Horsetail*

Courage

to follow the dictates of Divine purpose—*Cattail Pollen*
in the face of conflict—*Prickly Wild Rose*
to let one's true self be seen by others—*Monkshood*
to pioneer the way for others to follow—*Aventurine, Yellow Dryas*

Creativity

sharing one's creativity freely with others—*Wild Iris*
opening up new levels of creative expression—*Northern Lights, Sticky
Geranium*
owning one's diverse talents and traits—*Golden Corydalis*
recharging one's creative energy—*Carnelian, Liard Hot Springs, Opal,
Orange Calcite, Spectrolite*
helps one tap into one's inner truth, joy, and wisdom as a source of creative
power—*Gold*

Death & Dying

for the shock and trauma of ending up in the hospital after an accident or
stroke—*Cotton Grass, Soul Support*
for finishing up past cycles of experience—*Blue Elf Viola, Labrador Tea,
Mountain Wormwood, Sitka Burnet, Sphagnum Moss*
for a fear of dying—*Bog Rosemary, Chiming Bells, Tundra Rose*

Death and Dying (cont.)

for making the decision to cross over, and to assist in that journey—
*Bladderwort, Cattail Pollen, Round-Leaved Sundew, Hairy Butterwort,
Ladies Tresses, Shooting Star, Spiraea*

for protection after leaving the body—*Guardian, Angelica*

Dental Care

releasing emotional energy stored in the teeth—*White Fireweed*

support before, during and after a dental appointment—*Cotton Grass,
Fireweed Combo, Soul Support*

Depression

from lack of light—*Lighten Up, Orange Calcite, Solstice Sun*

for those who feel lost or out of touch with their own inner dynamics—
Chiming Bells

for those feeling separate and alone in times of darkness—*Single Delight*

Detoxification

release of toxic energy from the mind, emotions, physical body, and from
one's environment—*Black Tourmaline, Portage Glacier, Purification,
Smoky Quartz*

during and after a long flight—*Travel Ease*

Earth Healing

helps to rebuild the etheric web in areas disturbed or devastated by natural
or human causes—*Chiming Bells, Cotton Grass, Fireweed, Rhodolite
Garnet, River Beauty, White Fireweed*

Ego

relinquishing inappropriate identification with the ego—*Sitka Spruce
Pollen*

bringing the ego forces into harmony with the wisdom of the higher self—
Round-Leaved Sundew

Emergence

allowing issues to emerge into one's heart for healing—*Green Bog Orchid,
Sphagnum Moss*

Emergence (cont.)

allowing one's creativity to emerge gracefully—*Wild Iris*

helps suppressed issues emerge into the light of awareness—*Full Moon Reflection*

Emergency

maintaining physical balance during and after an emergency—*Cotton Grass, Fireweed, Labrador Tea*

regaining emotional balance after an emergency—*River Beauty, White Fireweed*

maintaining emotional boundaries during and after an emergency—*Covellite, Hematite, Tiger's Eye*

maintaining mental balance during and after an emergency—*Bunchberry, Citrine*

maintaining balance on all levels during and after an emergency—*Soul Support*

Empowered/Empowerment

from a clear vision of one's personal truth—*Cattail Pollen*

helps one maintain a strong sense of self when dealing with powerful emotions—*Hematite, Tiger's Eye*

empowerment through knowing and feeling one's true value—*Gold*

remaining true to one's values despite peer pressure—*Pyrite*

Energy

attracting and focusing energy for healing and regeneration—*Fireweed, Lady's Slipper*

expanding our ability to receive energy from the sun—*Lighten Up, Orange Calcite, Solstice Sun, Sunflower*

opening energy flows to and from the etheric body—*Fluorite, Fluorite Combo, Sweetgrass*

increasing energy flow to the meridians—*Carnelian*

opening energy flows to the heart—*Alpine Azalea, Calling All Angels, Chrysocolla, Emerald, Foxglove, Green Bog Orchid, Green Fairy Orchid, Harebell, Rhodochrosite, Rose Quartz, Sphagnum Moss, Tundra Twayblade*

Environment

cleansing one's environment—*Black Tourmaline, Grass of Parnassus, Portage Glacier, Purification, Sweetgrass*

removing static charges of energy from one's environment—*Solstice Storm*

helps one not take on the energy of the environment—*Guardian, Yarrow*

Etheric

breaking up and releasing blockages from the etheric body—*Fireweed, Fluorite, Fluorite Combo, Portage Glacier, Purification*

bathes the etheric body with multi-spectrum light—*Opal, Spectrolite*

rebuilds the etheric web of energy in areas disrupted by surgery or injury—*Rhodolite Garnet, Sweetgrass*

Exhaustion

from overuse of mental and emotional forces—*Opal, Spectrolite*

from trying to balance one extreme with another—*Labrador Tea*

from not resting—*Opium Poppy*

resulting from blockages in the subtle bodies—*Carnelian, Fluorite, Ruby, Sweetgrass*

Father

strengthening the father principle, in men and women—*Citrine, Sitka Spruce Pollen, Solstice Sun, Sunflower*

forgiveness—*Mountain Wormwood*

Fear

of the misuse of power—*Soapberry*

of flying—*Soul Support*

relating to the world with fearlessness—*Monkshood*

release of fear through trust—*Bog Rosemary*

overcoming fears of death—*Chiming Bells, Tundra Rose*

releasing fear from the heart—*False Hellebore, Forget-Me-Not, Foxglove, Rhodochrosite*

fear of the unknown, afraid to take risks—*Aventurine, Peridot*

fear of the power of nature—*Soapberry*

Feminine

opening up to a greater awareness of the feminine in nature—*Paper Birch*

balancing masculine and feminine energies in the heart—*Green Fairy Orchid*

blending the power of the feminine with the power of the masculine—*Sitka Spruce Pollen*

reconnecting to the wild feminine—*Green Jasper*

helps one embody feminine qualities of spirituality—*Sugalite*

opening to receive healing through infinite gentleness—*Northern Lady's Slipper*

opening to the nurturing energies of the Divine Mother—*Emerald*

Flexibility

helps one embody an attitude of flexible mind and resilient understanding—*Willow*

mental flexibility—*Chrysocolla, Lamb's Quarters, Wild Rhubarb*

gaining increased flexibility through the release of emotional blockages from the body—*Dandelion*

Flying

protection from electromagnetic radiation, noise and vibration during flight—*Travel Ease*

fear of flying—*Soul Support*

disorientation, jet lag—*Brazilian Quartz, Smoky Quartz, Travel Ease*

Focus

creating a positive focus for personality growth—*Golden Corydalis*

maintaining a spiritual focus in life—*Icelandic Poppy*

focused release of creative energy—*Sticky Geranium, Wild Iris*

focused release of resistance—*Greenland Icecap*

increasing one's mental focus by bringing the mind into alignment with Divine will—*Bunchberry*

helps a practitioner focus and direct energy for healing—*Lady's Slipper, Northern Lady's Slipper*

focusing our awareness in order to sense subtle energies residing in nature—*Northern Twayblade*

maintaining focus in one's healing process when many issues are coming up for consideration—*Fluorite Combo*

Forgiveness

of old wounds in relationships—*Mountain Wormwood*
through a clean and appropriate expression of anger—*Blue Elf Viola*
through acceptance of self—*Alpine Azalea*

Freedom

through healing the past on all levels—*Sitka Burnet, Sweetgrass*
through forgiveness—*Mountain Wormwood*
from injury and risk through a harmonious relationship with the Earth—
Pineapple Weed

Gardening

helps transplanted seedlings establish new roots of communication with
the Earth—*Grove Sandwort, Peridot*
helps build up the life force in the garden—*Moschatel, Orange Calcite,
Soapberry, Solstice Sun, Sunflower*
helps one tune into the needs of the plant kingdom—*Moschatel*
helping plants recover from frost or animal damage—*Soul Support*
opens one's awareness to the plant kingdom—*Comandra, Green Bells of
Ireland, Green Bog Orchid*

Grounding

grounding old energy patterns from the body—*Fireweed, Glacier River*
helps one release resistance to being fully grounded on the physical
plane—*Bloodstone, Brazilian Quartz, Rainbow Glacier*
strengthens the connection between the 1st chakra and the Earth—*Black
Tourmaline, Ruby*
helps one ground an awareness of life purpose into practical, heart centered
action—*Sapphire/Ruby*
grounding spiritual truth into the physical dimension—*Chalice Well,
Citrine*
connecting to place—*Cow Parsnip*
grounding communication—*Azurite*
reconnecting to the Earth after a shock or trauma—*Fireweed, Green Jasper*
reconnecting to the body after a traumatic experience—*Cotton Grass,
Rhodolite Garnet*
strengthens grounding on all levels—*Malachite*

Guidance

establishing connections with inner sources of guidance—*Horsetail, Monkshood*

awareness of guidance and support from spiritual sources—*Black Spruce, Moldavite, Shooting Star, Star Sapphire*

developing a greater trust in one's inner guidance—*Bog Rosemary, Hairy Butterwort*

balancing ego forces with higher guidance—*Round-Leaved Sundew*

Harmony

between mothers and children, children and the Earth—*Grove Sandwort, Pineapple Weed*

between human power and the power of the Earth—*Soapberry*

between the heart chakra and the green energy frequency of the planet—*Chrysoprase*

between the mental body and higher spiritual laws—*Citrine*

between personal and Divine will—*Diamond, Jacob's Ladder*

between the four levels of being: physical, emotional, mental, spiritual—*Malachite*

harmonizing the auric field and the physical body to the Earth's natural vibration—*Brazilian Quartz, Smoky Quartz*

Heart

opening our hearts to the experience of Unconditional Love from within—*Harebell*

opening the heart through unconditional self-acceptance—*Alpine Azalea*

developing the green, earthly dimension of the heart chakra—*Chrysoprase*

developing the pink, spiritual dimension of the heart chakra—*Kunzite*

releasing constrictions held deep in the heart— *Foxglove, Green Bog Orchid, Tundra Twayblade*

accessing information through the heart before interpreting it with the mind—*Lamb's Quarters*

core re-patterning of the heart energies—*Northern Lights*

clearing the channel of communication between the heart and mind—*Wild Rhubarb*

releasing muscle tension centered around the heart—*Foxglove, Soapberry*

experiencing the oneness of all creation through a deep cleansing of the heart—*Green Fairy Orchid*

Heart (cont.)

opening and expanding all dimensions of the heart chakra—*Chrysocolla*

opening the heart to allow a greater experience of love in the physical body—*Emerald*

increasing energy, balance, and stability in the heart chakra—*Montana Rhodochrosite, Rhodochrosite, Rose Quartz*

Higher Self

communicating with—*Jacob's Ladder, Tundra Rose, White Violet*

strengthening one's energetic connection with—*Brazilian Amethyst, Moldavite, Scepter Amethyst*

trusting in the wisdom of the higher self—*Brazilian Amethyst, Diamond, Gold, Hairy Butterwort, Round-Leaved Sundew, Scepter Amethyst, Sitka Spruce Pollen*

Homeless

for those who are drifting from place to place, with no place to call home, and who feel powerless to direct their lives—*Cow Parsnip*

Honesty

helps one make decisions based on an honest regard for one's highest good—*Paper Birch, Pyrite, Topaz*

willingness to see the truth of a situation—*Alder, Bladderwort, Cattail Pollen*

Identity

expansion and clarification of one's true identity throughout cycles of change—*Sunflower, Yellow Dryas*

building a strong projection of one's identity—*Columbine, Monkshood*

confidence from knowing one's true identity—*Tamarack*

strengthens one's ability to act from a clear sense of personal identity—*Carnelian, Topaz*

helps one access and bring forth the highest aspects of one's identity—*Gold, Scepter Amethyst*

Individuality

developing a conscious connection with the source of one's individuality—*Tamarack, Yellow Dryas*

Individuality (cont.)

helps one develop one's unique individuality—*Columbine, Lace Flower, One-Sided Wintergreen, Topaz*

Inner Child

gentle support for the healing of core traumas—*Emerald, Northern Lady's Slipper*

healing sexual issues—*Balsam Poplar*

release of anger and frustration from the inner child—*Blue Elf Viola*

moving the focus from pain to healing—*Cotton Grass*

getting back in touch with one's original innocence—*Forget-Me-Not, Liard Hot Springs*

directing healing energy to the inner child—*Lady's Slipper*

strengthening bonds of communication with the Earth mother—*Grove Sandwort*

helps one connect to and nurture one's inner child—*Rose Quartz, Sweetgale*

helps the inner child forgive and let go of past hurts—*Mountain Wormwood*

creating a place of safety within the heart—*Calling All Angels, Montana Rhodochrosite*

Integration

of eternal wisdom into present time awareness—*Black Spruce*

of spirit and emotion into action in the present moment—*White Spruce*

of new experiences by the personality—*Golden Corydalis*

of emotions—*Dandelion, Sweetgale*

of the lessons of the past—*Opium Poppy*

of the rational and the intuitive—*Lamb's Quarters*

of the celestial and the physical—*Rainbow Glacier*

of peak experiences—*Solstice Sun*

Intuition

opening one's intuition to the plant kingdom—*Comandra, Moschatel*

balancing the intuitive with the rational—*Lamb's Quarters*

increasing feminine aspects of intuition in men and women—*Moonstone*

trusting one's intuition—*Bog Rosemary*

Irritation

helps dissolve layers of irritation in the mental and emotional bodies—
Pearl

releasing irritation towards one's own healing process—*Sphagnum Moss*

Isolation

support for those who feel isolated from others—*Single Delight*

feeling separated or isolated from one's spiritual source—*Moldavite,
Sapphire, Shooting Star*

Joy

in physical existence—*Chiming Bells, Orange Calcite*

bringing more joy into the fulfillment of life's challenges—*Tundra Rose*

helps one tap into joy as a source of creative power—*Goatsbeard, Gold*

Judgment

learning to see without holding any judgment in one's heart—*Sphagnum
Moss*

helps turn judgment of one's difficulties into acceptance and awareness—
Pearl

release of conditions to loving and accepting the self—*Alpine Azalea*

Lethargy

feeling weighted down by life—*Lighten Up, Orange Calcite*

helps one move from lethargy to decisive and focused action—*Sticky
Geranium*

emotional lethargy—*Bloodstone, Moonstone, Sweetgale*

Life Purpose

creating energy boundaries that are in alignment with one's life purpose—
One-Sided Wintergreen

reconnecting with life purpose after a shock or trauma—*Ladies' Tresses,
Northern Lady's Slipper*

gaining a clear perspective on one's life purpose—*Paper Birch*

strengthening one's ability to act in alignment with life purpose—
Diamond, Sapphire, Sapphire/Ruby, Star Sapphire

Light

awareness of the omnipresence of light—*Single Delight*

opening to the light of creation—*Northern Lights*

bathes the entire energy system with multi-spectrum light—*Opal, Spectrolite*

strengthening one's inner light—*Yarrow*

receiving nourishment and healing from non-visible light—*Grass of Parnassus, Lighten Up*

opening the energy channels to receive more nourishment from sun light—*Lighten Up, Solstice Sun, Sunflower,*

amplifies one's ability to assimilate light at the cellular level of the body—*Herkimer Diamond, Orange Calcite*

support for bringing one's shadow self into the light—*Full Moon Reflection*

Limitation

releasing tension around the heart that has its source in mental patterns of limitation—*Foxglove*

dissolving limiting beliefs that restrict our experience of abundance—*Blueberry Pollen, Bog Blueberry*

going beyond previous levels of self-definition—*Sticky Geranium*

letting go of all limitations to receiving love from within—*Alpine Azalea, Chrysocolla, Emerald, Harebell*

Listening

from a place of inner quiet and focused neutrality—*Aquamarine, Twinflower*

to the subtleties of nature—*Cassandra*

clears confusion between hearing and knowing—*Lapis Lazuli*

Love

being motivated by a love of life—*Tundra Rose*

bringing Unconditional Love through the heart—*Alpine Azalea, Harebell*

opening the heart to allow a greater experience of love in the physical body—*Chrysocolla, Emerald, Tundra Twayblade*

opening the heart to an awareness and experience of angelic love—*Calling All Angels, Kunzite*

harmonizes the giving and receiving qualities of love—*Watermelon Tourmaline*

Manifesting

abundance on all levels—*Bog Blueberry, Blueberry Pollen*
a positive reality from the quality of one's thoughts—*Willow*
through a strong connection with one's creative power—*Gold, Wild Iris*

Masculine

strengthening the flow of masculine energy in men and women—*Solstice Sun, Sunflower*
balancing masculine and feminine energies in the heart—*Green Fairy Orchid, Watermelon Tourmaline*
balancing power and gentleness, in men and women—*Sitka Spruce Pollen*

Meditation

preparing oneself for meditation—*Horsetail*
getting in touch with life purpose when faced with difficult decisions—*Paper Birch, Shooting Star*
quieting the mind—*Aquamarine, Cassandra, Polar Ice*
cleansing a physical and vibrational space for meditation or ritual—*Grass of Parnassus, Purification, Sweetgrass*

Mother

strengthening the mother principle—*Grove Sandwort, Pineapple Weed*
opening the heart to the Divine Mother—*Chiming Bells, Emerald*

Motivation

opening to higher sources of motivation, especially in one's writing and speaking—*Tundra Rose*
balancing one's motivation with an awareness of what has already been accomplished—*Opium Poppy*
motivation from a clear awareness of purpose—*Paper Birch*

Nature

opening to the light and intelligence residing in nature—*Green Bells of Ireland*
learning to be nurtured and supported by nature—*Spiraea*
establishing bonds of communication with nature—*Cassandra, Grove Sandwort*
releasing fears of the power of nature—*Soapberry*

Nature (cont.)

awareness of the angelic kingdom in nature—*Alpine Azalea, Chiming Bells*
helps one feel at home in nature—*Chrysoprase*
awareness of the subtler aspects of nature—*Comandra, Moschatel, Northern Twayblade*

Newborn

helps newborn babies greet the Earth—*Green Bells of Ireland*
help in establishing bonds of communication with the mother and the Earth—*Grove Sandwort, Pineapple Weed*
support and protection for the newly born—*Covellite, Guardian, Peridot, White Violet, Yarrow*

Nurturing

learning to nurture and be nurtured unconditionally—*Spiraea*
supports the practice of nurturing between mother and child—*Grove Sandwort*
helps the inner child receive nurturing from the Divine Mother and from the Earth—*Emerald, Northern Lady's Slipper, Rose Quartz*
strengthens a nurturing connection between the Earth and the 5th chakra—*Azurite*

Opening

opening and maintaining a spiritual focus in life—*Icelandic Poppy*
opening one's heart to the spirit of angelic love—*Alpine Azalea, Angelica, Kunzite*
opening one's mind to the experience of abundance—*Blueberry Pollen*
opening channels of communication with higher sources of energy and information—*Lapis Lazuli, Rutilated Quartz*
to the omnipresence of light—*Single Delight*
to the active, masculine flow of energy—*Solstice Sun, Sunflower*
to higher sources of motivation—*Tundra Rose*
an intuitive connection with the plant kingdom—*Comandra, Moschatel*
opening energy channels to receive healing energy—*Lady's Slipper, Northern Lady's Slipper*
opening the heart to healing through trust—*Bog Rosemary*

Overwhelmed

by the amount of energy or information one is receiving—*Lapis Lazuli, Rutilated Quartz, Twinflower*

by the pace and intensity of life's changes—*Fireweed, Golden Corydalis, Greenland Icecap, Labrador Tea, Tidal Forces*

by energies from others or from the environment—*Black Tourmaline, Covellite, Guardian, Hematite, Yarrow*

Peace

through understanding one's true nature—*Chiming Bells, Jadeite Jade*

peace of mind during times of change—*Cow Parsnip*

peace from an awareness of Divine support—*Chalice Well, Hairy Butterwort*

Perception

of nature on a deeper and more profound level—*Cassandra, Comandra, Green Bog Orchid, Moschatel*

of the finer, subtler energies of spirit as they exist in form—*Northern Twayblade*

clarity of visual perception—*Alder, Herkimer Diamond*

releasing mental beliefs that limit one's perceptions—*Blueberry Pollen, Foxglove*

of the essential oneness of the universe through an open heart—*Green Fairy Orchid*

Perspective

opening to a more universal perspective—*Lamb's Quarters, Moldavite*

changing one's perspective from pain to healing—*Cotton Grass*

needing to restore perspective—*Foxglove, Paper Birch*

helps one learn a new perspective of balance—*Labrador Tea, Opium Poppy*

Power

harmonizing our personal power with the power of nature—*Soapberry, Solstice Storm*

blending power and gentleness—*Sitka Spruce Pollen*

tapping into one's inner truth and joy as a source of personal power—*Gold*

Pre-Menstrual

releases emotional tension, promotes circulation of emotional energies—*Bloodstone*

calms and soothes overly reactive emotional states—*Moonstone, Tidal Forces*

inconsistent and uneven flow of energy due to shock or trauma from the past—*Balsam Poplar, Green Jasper, River Beauty, White Fireweed*

Protection

from environmental pollution and toxicity—*Guardian*

for carrying out one's life purpose—*Cattail Pollen, One-Sided Wintergreen*

for the newly born—*Peridot*

for practitioners and healers—*Guardian, Lavender Yarrow*

being one's own source of protection—*Yarrow*

helps sensitive people create functional energy boundaries—*White Violet*

creating a sacred, protective space for deep inner work—*Monkshood*

adds clarity and definition to the auric field—*Covellite*

protection from other's negative emotional energies—*Hematite*

Purification

of the etheric body—*Fluorite, Fluorite Combo, Sweetgrass*

of one's immediate environment—*Grass of Parnassus, Solstice Storm, Sweetgrass*

of body, mind, and emotions—*Black Tourmaline, Portage Glacier*

of stagnant energy on any or all levels—*Purification*

Receptivity

to the angelic kingdom—*Angelica, Chiming Bells, Kunzite*

to one's spiritual power—*Brazilian Amethyst, Icelandic Poppy, Scepter Amethyst*

increasing mental receptivity by opening the channel between the heart and mind—*Wild Rhubarb*

developing emotional receptivity—*Sweetgale*

dedicating one's mental capacities to receiving the creative impulses of the soul *Jacob's Ladder*

creating functional energy boundaries to support one's receptivity—*Covellite, White Violet*

helps one move from over-sensitivity to centered receptivity—*Moonstone*

Regeneration

of the etheric body—*Fireweed, Fluorite Combo, Opal, Sweetgrass*
emotional regeneration after a traumatic event—*River Beauty*
physical regeneration through the healing of old wounds—*Cotton Grass, Fireweed, Rhodolite Garnet*
spiritual regeneration—*Brazilian Amethyst, Chiming Bells, Kunzite*

Rejuvenation

on all levels—*Fireweed, Liard Hot Springs, Portage Glacier, Spectrolite*
of spent emotional and mental forces—*Lighten Up, Opal*

Relationships

release of unforgiven areas in—*Mountain Wormwood*
opening emotional interactions in—*Sweetgale*
balancing communication in relationships—*Twinflower*
balancing one's relationship with the Earth—*Turquoise*
encourages mutual awareness and healing in relationships—*Full Moon Reflection*

Release

of emotional tension held in muscle tissue—*Dandelion*
of pain held in the body—*Cotton Grass*
of sexual tension stemming from experiences of abuse—*Balsam Poplar*
of self-doubt—*Alpine Azalea, Tamarack*
of emotional tension in male/female relationships—*Sweetgale*
of energy patterns that no longer serve us—*Fireweed, Northern Lights, Purification, Sitka Burnet*
of the fear of one's own power and of the power of nature—*Soapberry*
of a negative or false self-image—*Columbine, Lace Flower*

Releasing

the energy surrounding unresolved conflicts—*Blue Elf Viola*
pain held deep in the subconscious—*Forget-Me-Not*
emotional tension centered around the heart—*Foxglove, Soapberry*
the need to mentally control the events of our lives—*Jacob's Ladder*
deep patterns of limitation held in the mind—*Blueberry Pollen*
attachment to distraction—*Bunchberry*
resentment towards oneself or another—*Mountain Wormwood*

Releasing (cont.)

constrictions held deep in the heart—*Green Bog Orchid, Green Fairy Orchid*

judgment from the heart—*Sphagnum Moss*

old ingrained habits that are no longer useful—*Portage Glacier*

inner potential—*Sticky Geranium*

emotional shock—*White Fireweed*

deeply held trauma—*Ladies' Tresses*

mental resistance to change—*Blueberry Pollen, Glacier River, Greenland Icecap, Tidal Forces, Willow*

toxic patterns in an environment where there has been addition, depression, or abuse—*Purification*

Remembering

our original innocence—*Forget-Me-Not, Liard Hot Springs*

wisdom from past experiences—*Black Spruce, White Spruce*

Resilience

of mind—*Chrysocolla, Wild Rhubarb, Willow*

of body—*Dandelion, Pearl*

promotes a resilient attitude toward life—*Tidal Forces*

Resistance

to becoming fully connected with the physical plane—*Bloodstone, Rainbow Glacier*

to growth and expansion—*Spiraea*

to receiving love from universal sources—*Harebell*

to change and transformation—*Glacier River, Greenland Icecap*

overcoming mental resistance—*Willow*

overcoming resistance to being healed—*Bog Rosemary, Northern Lady's Slipper*

Responsibility

helps one take responsibility for why they have incarnated—*Sapphire*

taking responsibility for the reality that one has created—*Willow*

taking responsibility for one's personal power and how it is expressed in the world—*Sitka Spruce Pollen, Soapberry*

Restoration

of equilibrium and a nurturing flow of energy to the body after injury, shock, and trauma—*Cotton Grass, Fireweed, Soul Support*
of one's interest in life—*Prickly Wild Rose, Tundra Rose*

Seeing

through perceptual constrictions to the heart of the matter—*Foxglove*
with unconditional love—*Sphagnum Moss*
through illusion to the truth—*Bladderwort*
beyond our normal range of perception—*Alder, Herkimer Diamond, Northern Twayblade*

Self-Appreciation

of one's beauty, regardless of how it differs from other's—*Columbine*
of one's unique contribution to the evolution of humanity—*Lace Flower*
of our creative abilities—*Wild Iris*

Self-Esteem

from knowing one's abilities—*Tamarack*
strengthening self-esteem, especially with regard to group dynamics and peer pressure—*Pyrite*
from a clear sense of one's identity—*Gold, Tiger's Eye, Topaz*

Sensitivity

support and protection for those who are highly sensitive—*Covellite, Guardian, One-Sided Wintergreen, White Violet, Yarrow*
grounding one's sensitivity into physical experience—*Comandra, Northern Twayblade*
balances and harmonizes sensitivity during menstruation—*Moonstone*
lack of emotional sensitivity—*Bloodstone, Sweetgale*

Sexuality/Sexual Energy

synchronizing sexual energy with planetary cycles and rhythms—*Balsam Poplar*
restores earthly sensuality and healthy sexuality—*Green Jasper*
clearing negative programming around sexuality—*White Fireweed*

Shock

recovering from a shock to the physical body—*Cotton Grass, Fireweed*

recovering from a shock to the emotional body—*River Beauty, White Fireweed*

recovering from a shock to the heart—*Montana Rhodochrosite, Rose Quartz*

releasing shock that has been locked into the cellular structure of the body—*Ladies' Tresses, Tundra Twayblade, White Fireweed*

releasing shock from the etheric body—*Fireweed, Fluorite, Sweetgrass*

treating shock on all levels—*Soul Support*

Space Clearing

clearing and releasing—*Grass of Parnassus, Portage Glacier, Purification, Solstice Storm, Sticky Geranium, Sweetgrass*

maintaining energy flow—*Lady's Slipper, Tidal Forces*

invocation—*Calling All Angels, Chalice Well, Chiming Bells, Kunzite, Lighten Up*

preservation and protection—*Covellite, Guardian, Hematite, Peridot, Yarrow*

Spiritual/Spirituality

promotes recognition of the spiritual realm—*Brazilian Amethyst, Scepter Amethyst*

brings a depth and physical richness to one's spiritual life—*Sugalite*

supports the unfoldment of spiritual receptivity and radiance—*Icelandic Poppy*

helps one balance the flow of spiritual energies in the body—*Opium Poppy*

Strengthening

one's inner connection with infinity—*Bog Rosemary*

the bonds of communication between mother and child—*Grove Sandwort*

the flow of masculine energy in the body—*Sitka Spruce Pollen, Sunflower*

the flow of feminine energy in the body—*Balsam Poplar, Green Jasper, Lace Flower, Moonstone*

one's inner light—*Yarrow*

one's sense of self—*Columbine*

one's appreciation of self—*Lace Flower*

Strengthening (cont.)

the energetic boundary between one's emotional experience and one's true identity—*Tiger's Eye*

the heart chakra—*Chrysocolla, Chrysoprase, Emerald, Kunzite, Montana Rhodochrosite, Rhodochrosite, Rose Quartz*

Stress

relieving stress from the experience of extremes—*Labrador Tea*

letting go of emotional stress stored in the muscle tissue—*Dandelion*

stress from a preoccupation with mental activities—*Aquamarine, Jacob's Ladder*

Support

from the Angelic kingdom—*Angelica, Chiming Bells, Kunzite*

for any new cycle of growth and experience—*Peridot*

from all kingdoms and dimensions—*Chalice Well*

accessing Divine support in the moment—*Hairy Butterwort*

for those who are pioneering new realms, whether inner or outer—*Aventurine, Yellow Dryas*

unconditional acceptance of support—*Spiraea*

Surrendering

the power of the mind to the joy of the heart—*Lamb's Quarters*

the pain from old wounds—*Cotton Grass*

unforgiven areas in our relationships with others and with the self—*Mountain Wormwood*

inappropriate mental control over the events of life—*Jacob's Ladder*

to the timing of one's inner processes—*Greenland Icecap, Polar Ice*

Synchronization

of internal body rhythms with the natural cycles of the planet—*Balsam Poplar, Green Jasper*

of the auric field with the natural vibration of the Earth—*Brazilian Quartz, Malachite, Smoky Quartz*

of the movement of energy between the etheric and physical bodies—*Fluorite Combo*

gaining safety and freedom from risk through a synchronization of mind and body—*Pineapple Weed*

Transformation

letting go of resistance to—*Glacier River, Greenland Icecap, Spiraea, Tidal Forces*

of life patterns that no longer contribute to our highest good—*Fireweed, Northern Lights, Portage* Glacier

realignment of one's energy field with one's higher purpose—*Cattail Pollen, Ladies' Tresses, Sapphire, Sapphire/Ruby, Star Sapphire*

support during or after emotional transformation—*Chiming Bells, River Beauty*

support for the physical body during a transformation of any kind—*Fireweed, Rainbow Glacier*

support for when one feels stuck in the middle of transformative process—*Fireweed Combo, Hairy Butterwort, Sticky Geranium*

support on all levels during transformation—*Soul Support*

Transition

moving through a transition without the creation of crisis or illness—*Hairy Butterwort*

peace and contentment during times of transition—*Cow Parsnip*

patience during transition—*Polar Ice*

Trauma

topical application where there has been a trauma to the body—*Cotton Grass*

releasing trauma from all levels of the being—*Fireweed, Soul Support*

brings a balancing and centering influence during or after a traumatic experience—*Jadeite Jade, Labrador Tea*

helps with the process of emotional reorientation after a traumatic event—*River Beauty, Rose Quartz*

calming to the emotional body after it has suffered a recent trauma—*Emerald, White Fireweed*

release of trauma held in the cellular consciousness of the body—*Ladies' Tresses*

gentle release of trauma without having to re-experience it—*Northern Lady's Slipper*

healing trauma with unconditional love—*Tundra Twayblade*

healing trauma after surgery—*Cotton Grass, Rhodolite Garnet*

Travel

helps one travel through time zones more easily—*Black Tourmaline, Chrysocolla, Smoky Quartz*

helps one adapt to new surroundings more quickly—*Brazilian Quartz, Cow Parsnip, Green Jasper, Grove Sandwort*

letting go of stress and tension from traveling—*Dandelion, Labrador Tea*

for all aspects of travel—*Travel Ease*

Trust

in oneself—*Prickly Wild Rose, Pyrite*

deep cleansing and healing through trust—*Bog Rosemary*

creating new boundaries based on trust—*White Violet*

in the unknown and the unknowable—*Round-Leaved Sundew, Star Sapphire*

Truth

grounding higher truth into one's personal experiences—*Alder*

seeing through illusion—*Bladderwort, Diamond*

standing tall in one's own truth—*Cattail Pollen*

increases one's access to Divine truth—*Citrine*

building an energetic foundation for one's life based on one's highest truth—*Pyrite*

grounding spiritual truth into the physical dimension—*Chalice Well, Scepter Amethyst*

Vision

clarity of physical, mental, and spiritual sight—*Alder, Herkimer Diamond*

clearing inner vision so that one is aware of the presence of one's soul family—*Single Delight*

clarity of vision from inner knowing—*Bladderwort*

clarity of vision from a clear heart—*Green Fairy Orchid , Sphagnum Moss*

Will

bringing the power of the will into alignment with the heart and mind—*Bunchberry*

activation of personal will in its highest form—*Diamond*

balancing personal will and Divine will—*Round-Leaved Sundew*

Wisdom

accessing wisdom contained in nature and the collective consciousness of the planet—*Black Spruce, Turquoise*

integration and embodiment of wisdom from past experiences—*Opium Poppy, Sitka Spruce Pollen, White Spruce*

Part Eight

Appendices

Appendix A - Alphabetical Index of the Alaskan Stock Kits

Flower Essence Practitioner Kit

Flower Essence Practitioner Kit

Environmental Essence Kit

Gem Elixir Kit

Gem Elixir Kit

Appendix B - Alphabetical Listing of the Alaskan Research Essences

Research Flower Essences

Alaska Violet—*Viola langsdorfii*
Angelica—*Angelica genuflexa*
Bleeding Heart—*Dicentra spectibalis*
Bog Candle—*Platanthera dilatata*
Chocolate Lily—*Fritillary camschatcensis*
Cloudberry—*Rubus chamaemorus*
Combination Poppy—*Papaver sp.*
Comfrey—*Symphytum officinale*
Crowberry—*Empetrum nigrum*
Crystal Saxifrage—*Saxifraga escholtzii*
Devil's Club—*Echinopanax horridum*
Dwarf Fireweed—*Epilobium adenocaulon*
Enchanter's Nightshade—*Circaea alpina*
False Hellebore—*Veratrum escholtzii*
Goatsbeard—*Aruncus sylvester*
Ladies' Mantle—*Alchemillia vulgaris*
Lapland Rosebay—*Rhodendron lapponicum*
Lavender Yarrow—*Achillea borealis*
Lilac—*Syringa vulgaris*
Nootka Lupine—*Lupinus nootkatensis*
Pale Corydalis—*Corydalis sempervirens*
Pasque Flower—*Anemone patens*
Pink-Purple Poppy—*Papaver somniferum*
Potato—*Solanum tuberosum*
Purple Mt. Saxifrage—*Saxifraga oppositifolia*
Purple Poppy—*Papaver somniferum*
Red Elder—*Sambucus racemosa*
Red-Purple Poppy—*Papaver somniferum*
Reindeer Moss—*Cladina rangiferina*
Round-Leaf Orchid—*Amerorchis rotundifolia*
Self Heal—*Prunela vulgaris*
Starflower—*Trientalis europea*
Stinging Nettle—*Urtica gracilis*

Valerian—*Valeriana officinalis*
White Lupine—*Lupinus nootkatensis*
Wild Sweet Pea—*Hedysarum mackenzii*
Yellow Paintbrush—*Castilleja unalaschensis*

Research Gem Elixirs

Amazonite
Amber
Apophyllite
Aragonite
Cinnabar
Diopside
Green Garnet
Green Tourmaline
Green Tourmaline/Smoky Quartz
Labradorite
Larimar
Mangano Calcite
Raspberry Rutile
Red Quartz
Rose/Smoky Quartz
Silver
Star Ruby
Tourmalated Quartz
Vanadinite
Vesuvianite

Research Environmental Essences

Bog
Solar Eclipse
Stone Circle
Typhoon
Winter In August

Appendix C - Essences for the Seven Levels of Application

1) Getting Here

Brazilian Quartz•Cow Parsnip•Fireweed
Green Bells of Ireland•Green Jasper
Labrador Tea•Malachite•Pineapple Weed
Rainbow Glacier•Rhodolite Garnet
Shooting Star•White Violet

2) Emotional Awareness and Healing

Blue Elf Viola•Bloodstone•Foxglove
Full Moon Reflection•Greenland Icecap
Hematite•Pearl•River Beauty•Sweetgale
Tidal Forces•Tiger's Eye•White Fireweed

3) Physical Awareness and Release

Balsam Poplar•Black Tourmaline•Cotton Grass
Dandelion•Glacier River•Grass of Parnassus
Lady's Slipper•Portage Glacier
Ruby•Smoky Quartz•Sweetgrass
Tundra Twayblade

4) Healing The Heart/Attunement with Nature

Chrysoprase•Comandra•Emerald•Green Bog Orchid
Green Fairy Orchid•Lamb's Quarters
Moschatel•Northern Lights
Northern Twayblade•Soapberry
Sphagnum Moss•Wild Rhubarb

5) Relationships and Karma

Black Spruce•Columbine•Forget-Me-Not
Golden Corydalis•Lace Flower•Mountain Wormwood
Polar Ice•Single Delight•Sitka Burnet
Turquoise•Twinflower•Willow

6) Awareness and Activation of Life Purpose

Bladderwort•Cattail Pollen•Gold
Ladies' Tresses•Monkshood•One-Sided Wintergreen
Paper Birch•Pyrite•Sapphire/Ruby
Sticky Geranium•Tundra Rose•White Spruce

7) Spiritual Growth and Awareness

Alder•Alpine Azalea•Brazilian Amethyst
Chalice Well•Chiming Bells•Hairy Butterwort
Harebell•Jacob's Ladder•Kunzite
Scepter Amethyst•Star Sapphire•Sugalite

Appendix D - Research Essence Qualities

New Flower Essences

Alaska Violet *Viola langsdorfii* - supports us in finding the right energetic relationship with ourselves, others and the environment, especially in crowded situations; helps us create a quiet place inside where the flame of love and enthusiasm for our life's work can be nourished and contained; helps us share our joy as a gift for others.

Angelica *Angelica genuflexa* - promotes acceptance of spiritual support in all situations; helps us experience protection as coming from a certainty of our Divine nature.

Bleeding Heart *Dicentra spectibalis* - opens the heart to forgiveness, compassion, and loving kindness; helps us dissolve barriers in the heart to let another or ourself back in; helps us reintegrate and resolve the polarities of love and separation, joy and suffering, and self-acceptance and unworthiness that exist in the heart by opening to the experience of compassion for all beings, beginning with ourselves.

Bog Candle *Platanthera dilatata* - this essence works with cycles of initiation, death and rebirth. It offers a level of support that enables us to enter into an experience of spiritual transformation and rebirth, and emerge from that experience with a sense of new found wisdom rather than confusion, fear, shame or guilt. Heals tendencies towards destructiveness, degeneration, and degradation and helps us bring discarded aspects of ourselves back to the Light, to the embrace of Divine Love.

Chocolate Lily *Fritillary camschatcensis* - opens awareness of one's center and its connection to the wellspring or source of one's vitality; helps one learn new ways of using and containing one's life force so that it can build up over time; useful for when outside involvements or expressions are not in synch with what is present within.

Cloudberry *Rubus chamaemorus* - replacing low self-esteem with an awareness of one's inner value; opening to the true source of one's being and reflecting this outward for others to see; helps one recognize the light of purity deep within oneself.

Combination Poppy *Papaver somniferum* - balance at the core levels of one's being; unification of all energies in the body; helps one express one's unique abilities into the world and then return to one's center for reorientation and self ordering.

Comfrey *Symphytum officinale* - supports healing on all levels; heals the etheric body when there has been an injury in this or another lifetime; promotes the embodiment of higher spiritual energies and the expression of one's divine potential.

Crowberry *Empetrum nigrum* - stimulates awareness of cycles of light and darkness, internally and externally; enables us to hold these variations with respect and gratitude, rather than with attachment or aversion.

Crystal Saxifrage *Saxifraga escholtzii* - expands awareness of and lends energy to the process of personal transformation; helps one blend the creative power of thought, intuition, and Divine will within the heart to accelerate one's healing process.

Devil's Club *Echinopanax horridum* - clears ambivalence about being present on the Earth and in our bodies; helps us express our truth firmly and clearly from the heart.

Dwarf Fireweed *Epilobium adenocaulon* - for the transformation of unresolved issues that are held at the core of our beings; helps us release pain and trauma from the past.

Enchanter's Nightshade *Circaea alpina* - brings balance between the polarities of light and shadow, expansion and contraction; heals the imbalance that is created by too much exposure to the light; helps one find peace, protection, safety, and security in the shadow through the release of fear; for moving from isolation and separation to connection and union with all life; helps us release the magic of our potential.

False Hellebore *Veratrum eschscholtzii* - promotes the release of false concepts; catalyzes movement from the old to the new; helps us face our deepest, darkest fears.

Goatsbeard *Aruncus sylvester* - knowing joy through optimism; helps one shift one's focus to the positive; helps one create and manifest positive reality through a strongly focused intent of bringing the soul's light and energy into the body; helps those who are highly energized on the mental level to ground and focus that creative energy into physical manifestation.

Ladies' Mantle *Alchemillia vulgaris* - protection around one's relationship to the sacred feminine; opening to embrace the Goddess; heals the feminine connection between sensuality, creativity and divinity; assists men in balancing their relationship with the mother, the inner child, and with feminine power, in themselves and in others; promotes the release of sadness, despair, and grief held in the lower chakras.

Lapland Rosebay *Rhododendron lapponicum* - penetrating insight into the self and all of nature; seeing without distortion; brings a person back to their senses when they have been looking outside of themselves for answers; reminds us to look within for wisdom, knowledge, perspective, and direction.

Lavender Yarrow *Achillea borealis* - balances the flow of spiritual energy to the heart; heals the depletion that results from dissipated heart forces or a chaotic influx of energy through the crown chakra.

Lilac *Syringa vulgaris* - aligns the chakras so that they can more fully receive and embody Light; helps us gracefully raise the frequency of our energy fields.

Nootka Lupine *Lupinus nootkatensis* - helps us confront and address deep karmic issues that surface repeatedly for resolution; shows where our awareness needs to be focused in order to make the change.

Pale Corydalis *Corydalis sempervirens* - balances addictive and conditional patterns of loving; helps us see our relationships as catalysts for spiritual growth.

Pink-Purple Poppy *Papaver somniferum* - purity in form; helps one embody and project Universal Love through the heart; warming, soothing, and strengthening for the heart; allows one to return to an open-hearted state after a loss has occurred and one feels lonely and cut adrift.

Potato *Solanum tuberosum* - physical release; for thawing out incomplete cycles of experience that are being held in the body; encourages love and self-acceptance to penetrate into every cell of the body.

Purple Mountain Saxifrage *Saxifraga oppositifolia* - recognition, grounding, and embodiment of wisdom from the higher self; helps one tune into and make practical use of information from the frequency of Universal Mind; promotes discernment and differentiation when attuning to cosmic sources of information.

Purple Poppy *Papaver somniferum* - helps one maintain balance during rapid phases of evolution–when one's entire vibrational makeup is undergoing transformation; enables one to experience deep levels of integration and rest while allowing the transformative process to continue; helps one open to and embody new information from the higher self that enhances life in the physical dimension.

Red Elder *Sambucus racemosa* - for contracting overly expanded states of being; helps us view life from the center rather than from the periphery.

Red-Purple Poppy *Papaver somniferum* - for balancing extremes between physical and etheric frequencies of energy; helps one focus on both the survival and spiritual aspects of life in a balanced way; supports one in making full use of one's physical capacities to embody spirit.

Reindeer Moss *Cladina rangiferina* - opens awareness of the continuum–the constant and eternal nature of life; promotes a greater understanding of our collective history on the planet and how we fit into the whole. This essence is for healing the collective loss that resulted when the native peoples of the Earth had to move from their homelands to make way for the dominant cultures. It is for those who have suffered the loss of connection with place–the loss of the living relationship with the many kingdoms that create and maintain the homeland.

Round-Leaf Orchid *Amerorchis rotundifolia* - support to live more deeply in one's own heart and maintain that position in times of confusion and chaos; promotes equanimity, balance, and awareness of one's center; helps one get to and stay with the core of an issue without being distracted by all the energy at the periphery.

Self-Heal *Prunela vulgaris* - promotes self-esteem, self-acceptance, and an expansion of love and compassion for oneself; helps strengthen one's belief in the body's ability to heal itself.

Starflower *Trientalis europea* - a soothing and comforting energy of purity, refinement, and innocence; promotes individuality, involution, and free expression of self; helps one open a stronger vertical connection with Earth and spirit; strengthens one's ability to maintain one's sense of self in crowded situations regardless of competition for resources or lack of space; supports heart centered contact and inspired communication in groups–both the ability to speak from one's heart and the ability to welcome the preciousness of what others have to say.

Stinging Nettle *Urtica gracilis* - helps those who are highly sensitive stay connected to the Earth and to their feelings; promotes grounding and reorientation after being overwhelmed by too much input; enables one to absorb and process energetic information and input in alignment with one's capacity to integrate it; for those who have been hurt deeply in the past and have a tendency to sting and repel those they really want to be close to; helps to heal the alienation that comes out of the fear of being hurt again.

Valerian *Valeriana officinalis* - helps one slow down in order to gain perspective on priorities, especially when one feels under pressure to do or decide; promotes harmony in relationships; helps groups find a peaceful common ground.

White Lupine *Lupinus nootkatensis* - supports the emergence of a new archetype of male spiritual energy; helps men ground the energy of Spiritual Mastery; promotes the assimilation of one's destiny; stimulates the release of familial or tribal karmic patterns; promotes a willingness to release old patterns of behavior without reactivity or attachment to one's treasured wounds.

Wild Sweet Pea *Hedysarum mackenzii* - promotes confidence and ease in our interactions with others; helps us offer our best in service to others.

Yellow Paintbrush *Castilleja unalaschensis* - helps one release emotional frustrations and feelings of self-limitation that block one's outward expression; opens and cleanses the heart so that it may act as a focal point for the expression of one's creative energies.

New Gem Elixirs

Amazonite - enables us to find emotional strength through a joyful cleansing of old emotional burdens; helps us connect to the water element and to our ancient origins in water; facilitates a clearing of our hearts and emotional bodies so that we can communicate more easily with other living beings.

Apophyllite - brings horizontal balance to those who are too vertical; improves the flow of emotional communication through the heart; opens and softens the heart chakra and brings balance to those who have an excess of energy focused in the head; helps us relax and share what we have; enables us to interact more freely with the water element, both within us and around us.

Aragonite - helps one be fully present and energetically connected to the Earth, spirit, and another person during healing work, and then facilitates the release of interpersonal energy connections so that both people can return to a state of energy independence; for those who work in other dimensions and have difficulty coming back into psychic balance on the physical plane; promotes energetic hygiene; helps us learn not to receive energy or information from another that is not our responsibility or in our highest good.

Cinnabar - stimulates the clearing of ancient karmic energy stuck in the lower chakras and in the subtle bodies of the Earth; works with feet chakras to increase the flow of energy coming from the Earth into the legs and up into the body; brings awareness to issues we have about our relationship with the Earth that keep us from receiving the energy we need to sustain our physical bodies; helps us release pain and deep emotional sadness stored in the lower chakras.

Diopside - releases self-destructive programming from the survival (1st) chakra; thaws out crystallized levels of fear, anger, and self-worthlessness that block the heart from accepting higher levels of consciousness and Divine Will; releases alienation and helps one rebuild trust and intimacy with all kingdoms of life; increases flexibility and exchange within the heart; support for moving through the density of grief and the sadness of separation.

Green Garnet - calming and soothing; anchors a person's energy, focus and consciousness onto the Earth plane; facilitates vertical grounding and horizontal stability; works with the two-way flow of energy and information between the heart and first chakra; helps one have a softer and more intimate relationship with the Earth; helps one bring more Earth energy into the lower chakras.

Green Tourmaline - a transparent stone that helps us see through the illusion of separation and experience oneness with life; lifts the veil between the human and natural world so that we can see ourselves reflected in all of life, and feel all forms of life within ourselves.

Green Tourmaline/Smoky Quartz - expands the downward flow of energy between the fourth chakra and the Earth; helps us release energies into the Earth that are no longer necessary; facilitates the evolution of our creativity through the development of the heart and our relationships with others and the Earth; helps us focus our creative energies as an effortless giving from the heart; promotes concentration and firm willingness in the creative act.

Labradorite - helps one attract, gather, and anchor the energetic nourishment of light into the body, especially into areas of blockage; replenishes those who have become depleted from using up their own energy reserves; good for those experiencing a light deficiency (Seasonal Affectedness Disorder) and for those who spend long days indoors; for issues of magnetism and attractiveness; helps one learn how to be responsible and conscious about their attractiveness and the energy they project.

Larimar - this stone holds the energy of nonviolence, safety, and nurturing; builds up a resonance in the emotional body that attracts and holds the energy of harmlessness and peace; helps one relax and receive nurturing without struggle; helps women feel safe in the feminine; helps men and women allow their inner masculine to serve the inner feminine; for strengthening the sense of Sisterhood between all women, the feminine, and the Goddess.

Mangano Calcite - a gentle, soft, and protective energy that helps one experience absolute safety in the heart; works with the inside dimension or structure of the heart chakra to create a safe, womb-like matrix for healing; gives strength and support for maintaining a compassionate presence in the midst of emotional pain, helps people move from fragmentation and separation to unity, and to also feel unity in separation.

Raspberry Rutile - prepares the seventh chakra to accept information from higher sources; helps translate fourth dimensional energies into the third dimension; helps us ground energy back into the body after a shocking or traumatic experience; facilitates the flexible and fluid movement of energy between the 8th chakra and the heart.

Rose/Smoky Quartz - synchronizes the heart with the Earth's vibration and with the frequency of love; helps one move energy from shadow to acceptance; facilitates the clearing and releasing of dense energy from the heart and body through grounding, self-acceptance, and an awareness of divine protection.

Silver - helps to restructure the physical and energetic bodies in alignment with universal intelligence and wisdom; anchors the infinite structure of Divinity in the heart; heightens awareness of the grace that resides within our own beings; promotes the balanced release of toxic energy from the aura; strengthens and balances the flow of energy from Divine Will through the heart and throat chakras and back again to the Divine.

Star Ruby - promotes heightened awareness and sharp focus in the present moment; helps one to draw, attract, and anchor energy and information into the physical body, where one is; helps ground those who stray off in their thoughts, who go into their heads or out of their bodies; balances both vertical and horizontal energy flows within the body; penetrates one's resistance to being present; good for those who are easily distracted, or who purposely maintain distraction in their lives.

Tourmalated Quartz - clears congestion to facilitate a balanced flow of energy and information to, from, and between the chakras; draws off excesses of energy from all chakras and subtle bodies and the physical body; balances the base chakra in its relationship to the higher chakras; helps with the initial breaking up or shattering of a stuck pattern and can be used at the end of a healing process to carry off any remaining energetic debris.

Vanadinite - helps us regulate and direct the fire element; for those who have an abundance of fire it brings an awareness of how to use it; for those who are depleted, it helps attract more through awareness; promotes flexibility and a willingness to release attachment during a transformative process; helps one transcend pain through a stronger identification with the limitless Self, rather than with the personality or the small self that is experiencing the pain.

Vesuvianite - brings an awareness of how to ground love from the higher dimensions into physical form; helpful for those who are experiencing difficulties in forming deep heart-centered loving relationships; connects us to the brilliant, purifying, energizing aspects of fire; helps us embrace our inner heat and vibrancy—to sit with confidence as the creator of our world.

New Environmental Essences

Bog - this essence was made in the Stepstone Bog near Kachemak Bay in south central Alaska. Bogs are semi-swampy habitats that harbor a rich diversity of plant and insect life. They hold the fresh new energy of potential and are alive with an abundance of elemental energies. On a vibrational level, bogs are special containers for the heart energy of the planet. They also represent freedom, joy, and adventure–the freedom of wilderness, wildness, and wide open spaces. Their healing gift to the human kingdom is to help us prepare and expand the spaces we hold for new experience, to help us learn what is it like to live with an open heart and a spacious mind. The Bog Essence represents a place of special connection with the Earth Mother. The Earth is pregnant with wisdom, potential, fresh energy, and new beginnings, all held in an enormous heart space. This essence is about potential–not only the realization of potential, but also for the ability to hold potential for new creation. It can be used to support any creative act, but it is especially applicable for women, to help them hold the feminine heart space as a chalice for creating new life, and as a source of nurturing energy for their families.

Solar Eclipse - this essence was made in the northern interior of Alaska during the solar eclipse of 7/21/90. It is an essence for balancing and harmonizing the feminine and masculine energies in men and women and for the conscious empowerment of the inner male, especially where an imbalance exists due to dominant female energy. This essence is helpful in situations where the mother took on the responsibility for all aspects of a child's development because the father was incapable or absent, or because she was unwilling to share this responsibility with the father or relinquish her control over the child in later years. In such cases, the individual must eventually break free of the eclipsing energy of the mother and at the same time learn how to develop his or her own masculine qualities. The Solar Eclipse essence facilitates this process by working with the person to balance their inner masculine/feminine dynamic. It does this by bringing one's focus and awareness to what the inner male requires for healing and balance, and by helping one access the fortifying energy of the Sun.

Stone Circle - this essence was prepared within a naturally occurring circle of stones located high in the Talkeetna Mountains of central Alaska. The formation of energy created by this circle of stones has immense healing power. It provides a protected space, a place to come back to after journeys and adventures for rest and nurturing. The energy of this circle can replace or replenish what has been lost through stress, misuse, and the trials and tribulations of living in the world. The Stone Circle essence is particularly useful for those who are working with balancing energy, especially those who are doing energy release processes with people (cord work, past-life work), buildings and houses (space clearing), and landforms (battle energy release). This essence creates an aura of solid protection in the energy field so that one does not take on any of the stagnant or unbalanced energies that one is called to assist in transmuting.

Typhoon - this essence was prepared during a typhoon on the Izu Peninsula of the island of Honshu in Japan. It was made with only rain water from the storm and some water from a local spring. Typhoon is about surrender, trust and cleansing. It teaches us how to surrender to the cleansing power of nature–a force that is much more powerful than we are–with enough trust to let this energy in without trying to block it in any way, so that it can do its healing work. The message of this essence is, "whatever you don't have anchored with purpose and intent is going to be carried away, so focus on what is important and let the rest go." Typhoon is a very penetrating essence that can work its way into our densest levels of resistance. It can also teach us about intensity–how to work with it in our lives, and how to co-create with it in nature.

Winter In August - this essence was made from melted snow and ice on the Greenland ice sheet during a snowstorm in the month of August. Winter In August is an essence for the clarification of identity and life purpose. It helps us determine our heart's path in life, and then supports us in clearing our minds, hearts, and emotional realms of all that is not contributing to the realization of true peace in our lives.